6/.

LIBRARY OF THE
UNION
THEOLOGICAL SEMINARY,
NEW YORK.

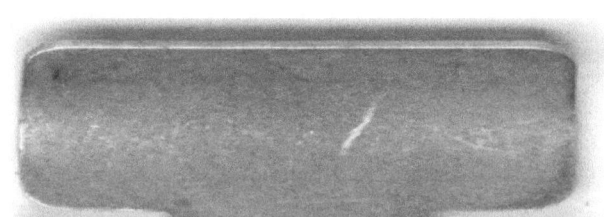

THE DOCTRINAL DIFFERENCES

WHICH HAVE

AGITATED AND DIVIDED

THE

PRESBYTERIAN CHURCH:

OR

OLD AND NEW THEOLOGY.

By JAMES WOOD, D. D.

The OLD IS BETTER.—Luke v. 39.

ENLARGED EDITION.

PHILADELPHIA:
PRESBYTERIAN BOARD OF PUBLICATION.
1853.

LIBRARY OF THE
Union Theological Seminary
NEW YORK CITY
PRESENTED BY
Thomas Samuel Hastings
NOV 14 1911

CONTENTS.

	PAGE.
INTRODUCTION to the Third Edition	5
PREFACE to the First Edition in 1838	15

CHAPTER I.
The character and government of God...... 25

CHAPTER II.
God's covenant with Adam and our relation to him as our federal head—involving the doctrine of imputation and original sin...... 41

CHAPTER III.
The subject of the preceding chapter continued—exhibiting the New Theology concerning God's covenant with Adam as the federal head of his posterity, imputation, original sin, &c...... 55

CHAPTER IV.
Remarks on imputation, original sin, &c. with reference to the views presented in the preceding chapter...... 71

CHAPTER V.
The sufferings of Christ and our justification through him 89

CHAPTER VI.
Justification—a continuation of the preceding chapter... 128

CHAPTER VII.

Human ability, regeneration, and the influences of the Holy Spirit.................................... 150

CHAPTER VIII.

Human ability, regeneration, &c. continued from the preceding chapter.................................... 173

CHAPTER IX.

A contrast between the Old and New Theology, by way of review, and a notice of the Perfectionism of Mr. Finney.................................... 193

CHAPTER X.

The measures adopted by the General Assembly for removing these errors from the Presbyterian Church.... 217

CHAPTER XI.

The acts of the General Assembly in 1837 and 1838..... 238

CHAPTER XII.

Present character and condition of the Old and New-school bodies.................................... 274

INTRODUCTION

TO THE THIRD EDITION.

The following treatise is designed to demonstrate that the issue between the two parties in the late controversy in the Presbyterian Church was strictly a doctrinal one. Hence the work consists mainly of a comparison of doctrinal views, as contained in the productions of Old and New-school writers. Near the close of the volume we remark, "It has been our aim, both in our statements and quotations, to exhibit the doctrines of the New Theology, just as they are, without the least exaggeration. For this purpose our extracts from New-school authors have been numerous, and sufficiently extended as to length, to give a correct view of their sentiments. But if it can be made to appear that we have misrepresented their views in a single important point, we shall cheerfully rectify the mistake." The first edition was published in 1838; and the second in 1845. It has been circulated widely; but up to the present time, (1853), no refutation has been attempted and no corrections proposed. Is not this silence a virtual admission of the fidelity of our quotations, and the essential verity of our statements? It has been denied, indeed, that the New-school Presbyterians as a *body*, maintain the errors imputed to them by their Old-school brethren; and yet the existence of those errors *among* them, they themselves acknowledge.

In a volume recently prepared by a committee of

the Synod of New York and New Jersey, and published under the sanction of the Synod, entitled "A History of the Division of the Presbyterian Church in the United States of America," I find the following: "Before a refutation is attempted of the charges of gross errors and irregularities against constitutional Presbyterians, justice to them requires that it be stated and borne in mind, that an overwhelming majority of them have *never denied* that there were errors in doctrine and irregularities in practice in the churches, which required correction. They believed there were, deplored their existence, and were willing to co-operate in the employment of constitutional and scriptural means for their removal. They then resisted and have uniformly borne their testimony against them. The evils complained of were mainly attributable to a class of reckless evangelists, and pastors who admitted them to their pulpits, some of whom doubtless approved and adopted their doctrines and measures." The exact *number* of those who embraced these errors, we have never professed to state. We did not know; and could therefore only say, that so far as we could infer from circumstances, we believed the number to be considerable. In 1838, we thought it probable they formed a majority of the new Assembly; but if we were mistaken, if "an overwhelming majority," were opposed to those errors, and "deplored their existence," it affords us the highest satisfaction to acknowledge our mistake. But whether they were few or many, their number was sufficient to disturb the peace of the whole church; and so influential as to render the ordinary method of church discipline ineffective and impracticable.

After the above admission of the existence of "errors and irregularities which required correction," and the declaration that they (the New-school) "deplored their existence," that they "then resisted and have uniformly borne their testimony against them," &c., we were prepared to expect that due credit would be given to their Old-school brethren for their laudable zeal in endeavouring to remove "the evils complained of;" however strongly they might object to the *measures* adopted for this purpose. But so far from this, the author of this volume, (strange to relate) does not give the Old-school Assembly credit even for sincerity in assigning doctrinal errors as the main ground of their proceedings in the case. The existence of errors exerted, according to his statement, a very subordinate influence in producing the alarm which was felt by their Old-school brethren, and in leading to those measures which resulted in a division of the church. The real cause of anxiety, it is alleged, was their waning influence in the church, by the rapid increase of the New-school party; and their urgency for final action arose from a determination to gain a permanent ascendency by excluding a portion of those who stood in their way. The proof of this, as adduced in this volume, consists mainly of a historical statement concerning the controversy with regard to benevolent operations—the Old-school believing it to be the duty of the Presbyterian Church in her organized capacity, to carry on the work of missions, &c.; and the New maintaining that this work could be prosecuted more efficiently by voluntary societies, in the support of which all evangelical churches should unite.

It is not our purpose to give the history of this controversy. Before its termination, it had assumed a serious aspect, considered merely as a question of benevolent action. It had come to this—not whether ecclesiastical boards are preferable, but whether they should be tolerated, our New-school brethren made repeated efforts from 1828 to 1831, to secure a vote of the Assembly, and the consent of the church at large, to merge the Board of Domestic Missions in the American Home Missionary Society; and in 1836, they refused (being a majority of the Assembly that year) to ratify the contract entered into the year previous, with the Synod of Pittsburgh, by which the Western Foreign Missionary Society, which had been conducted by the latter body, was to become the Assembly's Board of Foreign Missions. This refusal is denominated in the volume before us, a "signal defeat" of the "ultraists;" meaning the Old-school minority in the Assembly. If then, as is alleged, there was on the part of the latter, "a contest for *power*," it was for the power of *choice* in regard to the channel through which their benevolence should flow; the power to exercise their *Christian liberty* as to the mode in which they should endeavour to promote evangelical religion in our country; the power to act according to the dictates of their *own consciences* in having our branch of the church enrolled as a distinct and organized body among the hosts of the Lord, while engaged in fulfilling the Saviour's last command, "Go ye into all the world and preach the gospel to every creature."

But though this was a matter which was justly deemed to be of great importance, it might have been adjusted, if nothing else had been involved in it. With regard to Domestic Missions, a compromise was effected in 1831, and acquiesced in by both parties. But it was perceived that the difficulty lay deeper than this—that the foundation of their disagreement with regard to Ecclesiastical Boards, was a discrepancy in doctrinal views; and that the evil, instead of being remedied by concession or delay, would be likely to increase, through the influence of new Presbyteries, which would be formed under the Plan of Union, and the operation in our bounds of those societies, which had now become, in the hands of our New-school brethren, a powerful instrument to control the policy and modify ["Americanize"] the character of the church. If, again, there was, on the part of the Old-school, a "contest for *power*," it was for the power of preserving the *purity of the gospel*, as expressed in our Confession of Faith; and of maintaining a wholesome and necessary discipline of those who had introduced into our heritage strange and unscriptural doctrines. If, as this volume asserts, our New-school brethren "were willing to co-operate in the employment of constitutional and scriptural means for their removal," how did it happen that in every case of judicial process which came before the Assembly, on charges of doctrinal errors, they took sides with the accused! under the convenient plea that latitude in doctrinal belief was authorized by the Adopting Act of 1729, and that the errors charged were not "*fundamental;*" as though any doctrine, the belief of which does not absolutely peril our personal salvation, may be held and preached in our church without censure. This may be regarded as *liberal;* but in our judgment, it is more so than is consistent with the precepts of the gospel, or compatible with the purity, peace and prosperity of the church.

But we have no intention of reviewing the work alluded to. The numerous documents contained in it are doubtless a faithful transcript from the records, and give of course, as far as they go, a true history of the case. If these had been published without notes or comments, no objections could be reasonably made to the book, either by Old-school or New. But the accompanying remarks are very different from the version which is given of those transactions by Old-school men. In the three concluding chapters of the following treatise, (10th, 11th and 12th—not published in previous editions,) we shall give our views concerning these matters, without any particular reference, however, to the "History" above noticed.

Though my observations and reasonings do not accord with those of New-school writers, I see no occasion for imitating some of them in the use of severe and opprobrious epithets. Our doctrinal differences form no apology for personal abuse. The term New-school, which we employ, is not designed as a reproach, but as a convenient and appropriate designation of a party, as distinguished from the other, who are commonly denominated Old-school. The writer of the volume which we have had occasion to mention, does not object to these terms, but endeavours to show that, by a strange misnomer, they are applied exactly opposite to what they ought to be. The manner in which they came to be employed is well known. The first issue in the late controversy was made in the case of the Rev. Albert Barnes, in 1830; and his published errors were made, five years afterwards, (1835) a ground of prosecution. Immediately parties were arrayed; one resolved to make him amenable for these errors; the other equally resolved to defeat the attempt and hold him guiltless. During the protracted controversy which followed, the conflicting points of two materially variant systems of theology were brought prominently to view. The question was, Shall the doctrinal symbols of the Presbyterian Church be maintained in their integrity, or shall every one be allowed to interpret them according to his own caprice? The party maintaining these standards, agreeably to their obvious and long settled meaning, were soon and justly characterized as the Old-school; while that which contended for latitude of interpretation, and the allowance of novel schemes of doctrine, were styled with equal propriety New-school. In drawing the lines of demarcation, it was never supposed or pretended that all the ministers, and especially all the people who placed themselves under the New-school array, really held the alleged errors of some of their party; but submitting to leaders who did hold them, or who gave them their countenance, by shielding such as had deserted the old landmarks, they necessarily acquired the same name. How far these reasons exist for appropriating to them this appellation at the present time, will appear from Chap. xii. of this treatise.

We see no cause for altering the work as far as it was published in former editions, notwithstanding the allegation that we "quoted mostly from Congregational authors, with whom, on these points, the New-school Presbyterians have but little sympathy." This is a mistake. My quotations were mostly from authors who at the time of the publication of the books quoted from, were ministers in good standing in the Presbyterian Church; and with two or three exceptions they are now in the New-school body. Mr. Finney, though now a Congregationalist, was for some time a minister in the Presbyterian Church, during which period he preached with approbation in numerous Presbyterian pulpits in Western New York, the substance of those discourses which afterwards appeared in print; and their publication, for the most part, was prior to his leaving the Presbyterian Church. Since then he has published his "System of Theology," in which there is scarcely one trace of Calvinism; and the extreme views which he now maintains, he alleges, are the legitimate results of those doctrines. The proof which we adduced from Congregationalist authors, though indirect, was legitimate. New Haven was the foster parent of these errors; and the Quarterly issued there, from which our quotations were chiefly made, was not only read extensively by Presbyterian ministers, but was the medium through which one of them (the Rev. Albert Barnes) published some of his most objectionable matter. It was not from a conviction of its irrelevancy that Andover was not also referred to. As many of the ministers who sided with the New-school were alumni of the Theological Seminary at Andover, the sentiments of one of the Professors of that Institution might have been quoted with propriety, as tending to show the essentially anti-Presbyterian doctrines taught in that school. The late Professor Stuart, who, with that party, was a kind of oracle, repudiated, in some of its most important particulars, that form of sound words which has ever been the glory of the Presbyterian Church. His pupils undoubtedly adopted many of his peculiar sentiments. One of the present incumbents, Professor Park, has diverged still more widely from the doctrines of our church; and yet what New-school journal has condemned his errors, or cautioned their candidates for the ministry to avoid his teachings?

In an anonymous pamphlet which has just come into my hands, the design of which is to show that there is no essential difference between the doctrines of the two schools, my treatise is barely alluded to in two or three brief remarks, one of which is, that I misunderstand the New-school Presbyterians whom I quote. But as no intimation is given that my quotations are incorrect, it is not very material how I understand them. Every reader can interpret them for himself. My office was rather that of a compiler than an expositor. I submitted the question of agreement or disagreement to an intelligent and candid public; to be decided by an extended comparison of various authors. The decision has been made. Disinterested observers, whatever may be their creed, have been generally forced to admit that there are material variations in faith between the two bodies. No softening words, no extenuating pleas, no ingenious explanations can make the two systems one and the same.

But though we dare not attempt by the aid of nice, philosophical distinctions, to make those differences appear insignificant, we are equally indisposed to magnify their importance beyond what truth and candour require. It is to us a source of pain, and not of pleasure, to record the errors of Christian brethren; and we shall be sincerely gratified and thankful to God, when those which are noticed in this treatise shall be known only in history.

PREFACE

TO THE FIRST EDITION IN 1838.

IN numerous instances during the past year, the question has been proposed to me, "What is the difference between the doctrinal views of the Old and New-school?" Though several books and pamphlets have been written on a number of these points, and though most if not all of them have been discussed at various times in our periodicals, there are many in our churches who are not sufficiently informed on the subject, particularly in those sections where the new doctrines have not become prevalent, and where but few publications on the points at issue have been circulated. Recent occurrences render it peculiarly important that all in our connection should fully understand the merits of the question. It has now become a *practical* one. A decision is now being made whether we will continue with the church of our former choice, or unite with those who, without changing their name, have organized a new body. With a view of giving information to such as desire to ascertain on which side the truth lies, we shall present, in as concise a manner as the case will admit, the distinguishing features of the *New Theology*—comparing them, as we proceed, with those doctrines which have, by way of contrast, been denominated *Old*. For the sentiments of the Old-school we shall refer to the Confession of Faith of the Presbyterian Church and to standard Calvinistic writers. We think this cannot be reasonably objected to, even by our New-school brethren; since they have never charged the former with departing from the Confession of Faith. For the New-school doctrines, we shall make quotations from the professors at New Haven, Mr. Finney, and various ministers in the Presbyterian Church. We quote from those first named, because Dr. Taylor and his associates, though belonging to another denomination, are regarded as the *modern* authors of these speculations; and Mr. Finney, until within a few years past, belonged to our body, and preached and published most of his sentiments on these subjects before he left the church.

Some of the new doctrines began to be broached at New Haven in 1821–22, which created much dissatisfaction in the minds of a number who were made acquainted with the fact. In 1826 Professor Fitch published his *Discourses on the Nature of Sin*, and this was followed by a series of communications in the *Christian Spectator*, on the *Means of Regeneration*. The former were reviewed by Dr. Green in the *Christian Advocate*, and the latter called forth a controversy between Dr. Taylor and Dr. Tyler. In 1828 Dr. Taylor delivered his *Concio ad Clerum*, which was the cause of Dr. Woods writing his Letters addressed to Dr. Taylor; and the whole series taken together drew from Dr. Griffin his *Treatise on Divine Efficiency*, and led to the establishment of the East Windsor Theological Seminary.

Mr. Finney, who was hopefully converted and licensed to preach a few years previous, became celebrated as an evangelist in Western New York, in 1825–26. Though distinguished at first rather by "new measures" than by new doctrines, he soon adopted the views of Dr. Taylor; and he has probably done more to give them currency in certain sections of the church than any other individual. On some points he has gone further than his archetype; and on all perhaps has expressed himself with more frankness and less caution—asserting in positive terms what the former taught only by affirming that the *contrary* could not be *proved*. His lectures and sermons were the subject of animadversion in several periodicals; and as I happen to know, a certain minister seriously urged one of his (Mr. Finney's) co-presbyters to commence process against him; but nothing of this kind, I believe, was ever attempted.

In 1829 Mr. Barnes preached and published his *Sermon on the Way of Salvation;* which disclosed the fact that on a number of points he agreed substantially with the new system; and upon his being called, some months afterwards, to a pastoral charge in Philadelphia, some of the members of the Philadelphia Presbytery objected to receiving and installing him, on the ground that his sermon, which had been extensively circulated in that city, contained important errors in doctrine. The action of the Presbytery, Synod, and General Assembly, in 1830-31, the publication of his *Notes on the Romans* in 1835, and the charges and trials for heresy during that and the following year, are too familiar to all connected with our church, to need any particular notice. The preceding statements have been made merely to show the coincidence between the rise and progress of the new divinity in New England and its commencement and extension in the Presbyterian Church.

It has been said that the controversy in the Presbyterian Church does not respect doctrines at all, except as a secondary thing. Some have told us it is a strife for power—others a contest for the purse —and others a thrust at Congregationalism, and through that at New England. With whatever view these allegations have been made, the effect of them has been to produce distrust and disunion in many cases where there would otherwise have been a hearty concurrence in most if not all of the measures adopted for the reform of the church. This has been particularly the case with some whose partialities are strong in favour of New England. It would seem that such had forgotten for the time, that in New England the same controversy is going on which has agitated and ruptured the Presbyterian Church. If it is a war against New England, how does it happen that many of their ablest theologians have taken sides with the assailants? nay, that they were first in raising the note of alarm? The language of Dr. Green, in 1831, undoubtedly expresses the feelings of a large majority, if not of all the ministers in the Presbyterian Church. "'What!' we have heard it said, even by some who love us, 'What! are you arraying yourselves against the whole Theology of New England?' No—we have answered privately, and now answer publicly. No—we are arraying ourselves against Taylorism, and Fitchism, and Murdochism, and Emmonsism, and self-conversionism. But we thank God, this is not 'the whole theology of New England,' and we hope and believe it never will be. We know that there is a host of men, sound in the faith, who dislike and oppose most decidedly, this whole mass of error; and we hail these men, and love them as fellow labourers in the cause of truth, and bid them God speed with all our hearts."

Though in the progress of the difficulties some prominence has been given of late to Congregationalism, it was only from the circumstance that this was believed to have an important connection with the main question at issue. It is not the Congregationalism of New England that was the subject of discussion, but Congregationalism in the Presbyterian Church. Against Congregationalism, as such, there exists no hostility; but when, through the Plan of Union, it became the means, like the Trojan horse, of introducing into our body many who were unfriendly to our doctrines and government, it became necessary, in self-defence, to free the church from this improper, and to us, ruinous condition.*

The same remarks are applicable to the resolutions of the General Assembly concerning certain benevolent societies. Towards the American Home Missionary Society and the American Education Society, in their incipient stages, and *considered merely as organizations for doing good*, there was for a number of years the greatest cordiality. This is evident from the fact that they were repeatedly recommended by the General Assembly. But when it was found that their operations within our bounds, besides interfering with the free action of our own Boards, were made the instruments in the hands of those who managed the various Presbyterian auxiliaries, of increasing and extending our difficulties, and rendering them more unmanageable—the one by furnishing young men for our pulpits whose sentiments did not accord with our standards, and the other by directing and sustaining them in their fields of labour—the Assembly of 1837 withdrew their former recommen-

---

* According to the statement published by me, as corrected in the second edition, there are in the four disowned Synods three hundred and thirty-four churches nominally Presbyterian, and two hundred and eighty-six Congregational. A short time ago, a minister who was then a member of the Otsego Presbytery, observed to me, If you have reported as favourably concerning all the Presbyteries as you have concerning ours, they have no reason to complain. Instead of there being eight Presbyterian and eight Congregational churches as reported by me, there are, he said, but six Presbyterian churches and ten Congregational.

dations and requested them to cease operating in our churches. As in their action concerning the Plan of Union and the four Synods, so in regard to these societies, the ground of their proceedings was, that they believed them to be (to use their own language) "excedingly injurious to the peace and purity of the Presbyterian church"—and while they "hoped and believed that the Assembly would not be behind the protesters, [the patrons of those societies] in zeal for the spread of *divine truth*, they desire that in carrying on those great enterprises, the church may not be misled to adopt a system of action which may be perverted to the spread of error."

It is not true, therefore, that the controversy has little or no respect to doctrines. On the contrary, the principal and primary ground of it, has been a discrepancy in doctrinal sentiments. Its origin may be traced to the opinion so prevalent of late, among certain classes of men, that we ought to expect as great improvements in theology as have been made in the arts and sciences—that those formularies of Christian faith, which have been received for centuries as containing a correct statement of Scripture doctrine, are too antiquated for this enlightened age; and if received now, are to be explained agreeably to certain philosophical principles which were unknown in the days of our ancestors—and that the Bible itself is to be so expounded as to accord with those theories of mind, of free agency, and of moral government, which have been introduced by the new philosophy. It is this which gives to their theology the denomination of *new*. Considered chronologically, it is far from being new. Similar sentiments were advanced on most of the points in dispute, as long ago as the time of Pelagius, and they have sprung up and flourished for a while at different periods since. Were this the proper place, we could easily substantiate this remark by a reference to documents.

The principles upon which these modern improvements in theology profess to be based, appear to me to be radically erroneous. If the doctrines of religion were as difficult to be *discovered* by a diligent reader of the sacred Scriptures, as the laws and motions of the heavenly bodies are to an observer of the planets, the march of mind might be expected to be as visible in the development of new theological truths, as in the new discoveries of astronomy. But the Bible, I have always supposed, has recorded truth in order to *reveal* it; and not to place it so far beyond the reach of common observation, as to require the aid of a telescope to enable us to discern its character and proportion. Truth is immutable. The Bible is, therefore, not to be interpreted by a set of philosophical dogmas, which vary, it may be, with every successive age; but by a careful examination and comparison of its several words and phrases. These obvious way-marks were the same in the time of Augustine and Calvin, and the Westminster divines, as they are now; and it is by a faithful adherence to these, that so much uniformity has been preserved among Christians of every age, in regard to the doctrines of our holy religion. Abstruse metaphysical speculations have now and then held out their false lights, and led portions of the church into error; but whenever the pride of intellect and learning has been humbled by the Spirit of God, and there has been a return to that simple-hearted piety, which is willing to receive the plain teachings of the Bible, without stopping to inquire whether they are consistent with certain new modes of philosophizing, it has uniformly resulted in the revival of those old and venerable doctrines, which have been the stability and glory of the church in every period of her history.

We do not intend to convey the idea that all who are now denominated New-school, or who have united in organizing the new Assembly, embrace the new doctrines. Various reasons have operated to produce in the minds of some, so much sympathy for those who maintain these sentiments, that they have taken sides with them, and hence have received their name, though they disclaim all affinity for their peculiar views. Others receive the new divinity in a modified form; and a third class adopt some of its dogmas, while they reject others. These last remarks apply to some of those from whose productions we design to make extracts in the following pages.

How large a proportion of the new Assembly embrace the New Theology, we will not undertake to say. We might state a number of facts, which appear to show that it is adopted, at least, *"for substance of doctrine,"* by a very considerable majority. On the contrary, there are some who have expressed opposition to these doctrines, but who have been influenced, it is probable, by their local situation, or their connections and sympathies, to join the new body. Our earnest wish is, that they may exert a happy influence. We have no malignant feelings to gratify—but shall rejoice to know that every error has been corrected, every ground of complaint removed, that as a body, they may regain that Christian confidence, to which a few of their number are now so justly entitled. It is to be deeply regretted, that in one or two things they would not pursue a different course. Twelve months ago, a committee appointed by that party, consented to take another *name,* and to leave their brethren of the Old-school in the quiet possession of their records, board of trustees, and certain invested funds. An amicable division would doubtless have taken place at that time, had it not been for the fact that the committee from the New-school party, though they consented to the above reasonable terms, insisted upon such other conditions as could not be acceded to without jeoparding those very interests for the securing of which a division had become necessary. Hence the négotiation failed. But now they claim to be the true General Assembly of the Presbyterian Church, and have appealed to the civil courts to wrest, if possible, from the hands of their brethren, what, they virtually acknowledged a year ago, does not belong in equity to themselves, but to those whom they have thus assailed. Such a procedure seems to us grossly improper, as well as inconsistent. It is to be hoped, however, that on further reflection, they will be induced to retrace their steps and pursue a course more agreeable to their former professions and to the spirit of the gospel.

But while we do not doubt that these suits, if prosecuted, will be decided in favour of the defendants, provided law and *justice* do not conflict with each other, we wish to remind the reader that the question, which body is the *true General Assembly*, does not depend upon any decision which is to be made by the civil courts. They can decide who shall have the *funds;* but beyond this their jurisdiction does not extend. The General Assembly was organized ten years before they had a board of trustees; and their organization was as complete during that time as it was afterwards. It had then its constitution—and this constitution, be it remembered, makes the General Assembly, and not a civil court, the body of final resort in all cases of ecclesiastical jurisdiction. This board of trustees was incorporated for the purpose of managing certain funds in behalf of the Assembly, and for nothing else. If their charter had been a limited one, its expiration would not have affected the character of the General Assembly; and if it shall be taken away, the only result which can follow, will be to deprive them of their funds; but as an ecclesiastical body, they remain unimpaired. If they were the true General Assembly in 1789, and for the ten following years before their charter was obtained, they are the true General Assembly now, whatever becomes of their property.

Though we shall be gratified to have them succeed in this respect, we regard the result of these suits as of little importance compared with other matters which have been involved in the controversy, but which we trust are now finally settled. In regard to the question of property, we feel very much like a native Christian of the South Sea Islands who had lost his house by fire, and who in the act of rushing into the flames to secure a copy of the New Testament, was severely scorched by the conflagration. As the missionaries were condoling with him on the loss of his house, he put his hand under his garment, and taking out the sacred treasure which he had saved, exclaimed with ecstacy, "True, I have lost my property, but I have saved my gospels!" We may lose our property before the civil tribunals; but if we have saved our "gospels," we shall be infinite gainers, and ought therefore to "take joyfully the spoiling of our goods." These remarks are made in view of the prominence given in the New-school prints to a judicial decision: but we are far from believing that any professional ingenuity or legal skill will be able to procure such a result as they anticipate; even should they venture to bring the question to trial.

OLD AND NEW THEOLOGY.

CHAPTER I.

THE CHARACTER AND GOVERNMENT OF GOD.

In New England, the controversy on the subject of the present chapter embraces some propositions which have never been much discussed in the Presbyterian church, and concerning which the great majority of our ministers, we believe, have not expressed a decided opinion. We refer to the following, which we give in the language of Dr. Tyler: "Dr. Taylor maintains, contrary to my belief, that the existence of sin is not, on the whole, for the best; and that a greater amount of good would have been secured had all God's creatures remained holy, than will result from the present system." Again: "Dr. Taylor maintains, contrary to my belief, that God, all things considered, prefers holiness to sin, in all instances in which the latter takes place." It has been a common sentiment among New England divines, since the time of Edwards, "that sin is the necessary means of the greatest good, and as such, so far as it exists, is preferable, on the whole, to holiness in its stead." The sentiment is founded upon what has been denominated the

Beltistian Theory; which, it is said, was first taught by Leibnitz, about the commencement of the last century. This theory maintains, that "of all possible systems, God, infinitely wise and good, *must adopt* that which is *best*. The present system, therefore, is preferable to every other; and since sin is a part of the system, "its existence is, on the whole, for the best." Not that "sin must be good in *itself*," as Dr. Taylor disingenuously insinuates that they hold—this is no part of their belief—but that God will so overrule it, for the promotion of his glory and the happiness of the universe, "that a greater amount of good will result from the present system, than would have been secured had all God's creatures remained holy."* Concerning the principle of Leibnitz, from which these conclusions are drawn, Dr. Witherspoon remarks: "This scheme seems to me to labour under two great and obvious difficulties—that the infinite God should set limits to himself, by the production of a created system—it brings creation a great deal too near the Creator to say it is the alternative of Omnipotence. The other difficulty is, that it seems to make something which I do not know how to express otherwise than by the ancient stoical fate, antecedent and superior even to God himself. I would therefore think it best to say, with the current of orthodox divines, that God was

---

* New England *optimism*, as it is sometimes denominated, arises from the theory that virtue consists in benevolence—or that the tendency of holiness to produce happiness, is that which gives it its chief, if not its only excellence.

perfectly free in his purpose and providence, and that there is no reason to be sought for the one or the other beyond himself."

Admitting, then, that there was no *necessity* on the part of the Creator to form one particular system rather than another, it becomes merely a question of fact, whether more good will result to the universe from the existence of sin, all things considered, than would have been secured if sin had never been permitted. To this question, most of the ministers in our church, we are disposed to think, would reply by saying, "We cannot tell." All agree that "the existence of sin under the divine government is a profound mystery;" and also that God will make use of it to display some of his illustrious perfections; and to communicate to his creatures rich and eternal blessings. But whether he might not have formed a system, if it had been his pleasure, by which his glory would have been still more displayed, and a still greater amount of happiness secured to his creatures, it is not our province to decide. As he has no where told us that he has made the best system *possible*, and as we cannot perceive that his infinite goodness required him to do it, we are disposed to leave the question to be contemplated and solved, (if a solution be desirable,) when we shall have the advantage of that expansion of mind, that increase of knowledge, and that interchange of sentiment with other created beings, which we shall enjoy in the heavenly world.

But while in regard to these propositions we express no opinion, we consider the reasoning of Dr.

Taylor in attempting to refute them as involving pernicious errors. It is on this account that we have introduced the subject in the present volume. Pressed with the difficulty that if sin under the divine government will not on the whole be for the best, why did God permit it? he has taken the bold, not to say the impious ground, that God did all he *could* to prevent the existence of sin, but *could* not, without infringing on the moral agency of man—and that he would make the world holier and happier now if he *could*, without abridging human liberty.

His language on this subject is as follows: "It will not be denied that free moral agents *can* do wrong under every possible influence to prevent it. The *possibility* of a contradiction in supposing them to be prevented from doing wrong, is therefore demonstrably certain. Free moral agents can do wrong under all possible preventing influence."—*Christian Spectator*, Sept. 1830, p. 563.*

"But in our view it is a question whether it is not essential to the honour of God to suppose that he has done all he could to secure the universal holiness of his accountable creatures; and that nevertheless, some, in defiance of it, would rebel. Such a proposition we think neither violates the feelings of enlightened piety, nor the decision of revelation."—*Christian Spectator*, 1832, p. 567.

"God not only prefers on the whole that his

* As I have not all the numbers of the Christian Spectator in my possession, I shall, in my quotations from that work, make free use of a pamphlet written by the Rev. Daniel Dow.

creatures should for ever perform their duties rather than neglect them, but purposes on his part to do all in his power to promote this object in his kingdom."—*Christian Spectator*, 1832, p. 660.

"It is a groundless assumption, that God could have prevented all sin, or at least, the present degree of sin in a moral system. If holiness in a moral system be preferable to sin in its stead, why did not a benevolent God, were it possible to him, prevent all sin, and secure the prevalence of universal holiness? Would not a moral universe of perfect holiness, and of course perfect happiness, be happier and better than one comprising 'sin and its miseries?' And must not infinite benevolence accomplish all the good he can? Would not a benevolent God, then, *had it been possible to him in the nature of things*, have secured the existence of universal holiness in his moral kingdom?" *Concio ad Clerum*.

It is not surprising that the publication of such sentiments created alarm among the orthodox clergy of New England; and that speedy efforts were made to arrest their progress.

Unhappily, they soon found their way to New York, and through the agency of Mr. Finney and others, obtained considerable currency. Mr. Finney's views will appear from the following quotation. In reply to an objection that as God "is almighty, he could prevent sin if he pleased," &c., he observes: "To say nothing of his word and oath upon this subject, you have only to look into his law to see that he has done all that the nature of the case admitted to prevent the existence of sin. The sanctions of his law are absolutely infinite: in them he has embodied and held forth the highest possible motives to obedience. His law is moral and not physical; a government of motive and not of force. It is in vain to talk of his omnipotence preventing sin. If infinite motives cannot prevent it, it cannot be prevented under a moral government, and to maintain the contrary is absurd and a contradiction. To administer moral laws is not the object of physical power. To maintain, therefore, that the physical omnipotence of God can prevent sin, is to talk nonsense."—*Sermons on Important Subjects*, p. 58.

Similar language is employed by him and other writers of the same school with reference to the power of God to convert sinners, and to make the world holier and happier than it now is. Mr. Edward R. Tyler [not Dr. Tyler] preached a sermon at New Haven, Oct. 1829, (published by request,) in which occur the following sentences:* "He [God] does not prefer the present system to one which might have presented itself to his choice, had it been possible to retain all moral beings in obedience; but prefers it to the non-existence of a moral system, notwithstanding sin is its unavoidable attendant." "*The nature of things, as they now exist, forbids, as far as God himself is concerned, the more frequent existence of holiness in the place of sin. How do you know that the influence which He employs, even in respect*

* Mr. Tyler was at that time Pastor of the South Church in Middletown, Conn.

to those who perish, is not all which the nature of the case admits? How do you know that he can maintain his moral government, or preserve moral agents in being as such, and prevent sin? Do you not pass the boundaries of human knowledge in saying that he is able to prevent all sin, while he preserves, unimpaired, the freedom of accountable beings? Such may be the nature of free agents that they cannot be governed in a manner to exclude sin, *or to restrict it to a smaller compass than it actually possesses.*" "Such is the nature of free agents, that God foresaw he could not create them without liability to err and actual transgression. He knew at the same time, that the best possible system included such beings; that is, beings capable of knowing and loving him. He regretted, as he abundantly teaches us in his word, that some of those whom he was about to create would sin. Had it been possible to secure them all in obedience, more happiness would have been enjoyed by his creatures, and equal glory would have surrounded his own throne. But although the system which he saw to be best, could not be realized in consequence of the anticipated perversion of moral agency, he perceived a system such as he has adopted, notwithstanding the evil attending it, to be preferable to any which should exclude moral beings." "It is to him a subject of regret and grief, yet men transgress; they rebel in spite of his wishes; *they persevere in sin in spite of all which he* CAN *do to reclaim them.*"

A writer in the *Christian Spectator* [believed to be

Professor Fitch,] advances the same ideas. "Whatever *degree* or kind of influence" says he, "is used with them, to favour their return to him, at any given time, *is as strongly favourable to their conversion as it* CAN *be made amid the obstacles which a world of guilty and rebellious moral agents oppose to God's works of grace.*"—"Review of Dr. Fisk's Discourse on Predestination and Election."

In accordance with these sentiments, it was not uncommon, a few years ago, in some parts of New York, to hear from the pulpit and in the lecture-room, that God is doing all he *can* to convert and save sinners—that if he *could*, he would convert many more than he does—that he converts as many as he *can persuade* to yield their hearts to him—and other expressions to the same effect. Of very similar import is the remark attributed to a son of Dr. Beecher, which, according to the *Hartford Christian Watchman*, was *one* cause of Dr. Porter's anxiety in relation to the father—it having been reported that he approved of the sentiment, viz. "that though God is physically omnipotent, he has not acquired moral power enough to govern the universe according to his will."

How different these statements are from the old theology, will appear by a reference to the Confession of Faith; which teaches that God "hath most sovereign dominion over his creatures, to do by them, for them, and upon them, whatsoever himself pleaseth" —that he is "Almighty, most absolute, working all things according to the counsel of his own immutable and most righteous will, for his own glory." They are equally at variance with the word of God, which declares that "he doeth according to his will in the army of heaven, and among the inhabitants of the earth; and none can stay his hand, or say unto him, What doest thou?"

The positions assumed by Dr. Taylor and others, besides being unscriptural, are believed by many to involve principles which are subversive of some important Scripture doctrines. They place such limits upon the *power* of God, as to be a virtual denial of his *omnipotence*. They make him so dependent upon his creatures, as to render him liable to *disappointment*, and consequently to a *diminution of his happiness*. Dr. Taylor, or one of his friends, admits that his blessedness has been diminished by the existence of sin. "It is admitted that what men have done to impair the blessedness of God by sin, has not failed of its results in the actual diminution of his blessedness, compared with what it had been, had they obeyed his perfect law."—*Spirit of the Pilgrims*, Vol. V. p. 693. Mr. Tyler, who has just been referred to, makes the same admission. "This doctrine," he remarks, "is said to be inconsistent with the happiness of God. And we admit, that as far as his happiness is affected by the conduct of his creatures, he would have been better pleased had angels and men always remained steadfast in his fear and service."

They involve a denial of the divine decrees—for if God does not possess such absolute control over his creatures that he can govern them according to his pleasure, how could he have decreed any thing unconditionally concerning them, since it might happen, that in the exercise of their free agency, they would act contrary to the divine purpose? On the same principle they virtually reject the Calvinistic doctrine of election, and make election depend upon the foreknowledge of God and the will of the creature. This is actually the way in which Mr. Finney explains the doctrine. "The elect, then," says he, "must be those who God foresaw could be converted under the wisest administration of his government. That administering it in a way that would be most beneficial to all worlds, exerting such an amount of moral influence on every individual as would result, on the whole, in the greatest good to his divine kingdom, he foresaw that certain individuals could, with this wisest amount of moral influence, be reclaimed and sanctified, and for this reason, they were chosen to eternal life." "The elect were chosen to eternal life, because God foresaw that in the perfect exercise of their freedom they could be induced to repent and embrace the gospel." "In choosing his elect, you must understand that he has thrown the responsibility of their being saved upon them: that the whole is suspended upon their consent to the terms; you are perfectly able to give your consent, and this moment to lay hold on eternal life. Irrespective of your own choice, no election can save you, and no reprobation can damn you."—*Sermons on Important Subjects*, p. 224, 25, 29, 33. Mr. Tyler, from whose sermon we have already quoted, gives the same explanation of this doctrine, or, in other words, virtually denies it. "God foresees," he observes, "whom he *can* make willing in the day of his power, and resolves that they shall be saved." Prof. Fitch also advances the same idea in his review of Dr. Fisk's discourses on Predestination and Election, in the Christian Spectator.

The same remarks may be made, substantially, concerning the saints' perseverance, and even their stability in heaven. If the free will of sinners may effectually resist all the influence which God can use for their conversion, why may not the free will of Christians, under the counter influence of temptation, break through all the moral influences which God can bring to bear upon them, and they completely and eternally fall away? And if so, why may not the same catastrophe befall them after they arrive at heaven? To borrow the language of Dr. Tyler: "If his creatures are so independent of him that he cannot control them at pleasure, what assurance can he give us that every saint and every angel will not yet apostatize and spread desolation through the moral universe?"

Horrible as this thought is, it appears to be a legitimate consequence from the reasoning of the New Haven divines. "But this possibility that moral agents will sin, remains (suppose what else you will) so long as moral agency remains; and how can it be proved that a thing *will not* be, when, for aught that appears, it *may* be? When in view of all the facts and evidence in the case it remains true that it *may* be, what evidence or proof can exist that it *will not* be?"—*Ch. Spec.* 1830, p. 563. Again: "We know that a moral system necessarily implies the existence of free agents, with the power to act in despite of all opposing power. This fact sets human reason at defiance in every attempt to prove that some of these agents will not use that power and actually sin." *Ch. Spec.* 1831, p. 617. If, then, the saints and angels in heaven are "*free agents*," they have, according to the above reasoning, "the power to act in despite of all opposing power," and it cannot be proved "that some of these agents will not use that power and actually sin."

On this subject we will quote some pertinent remarks from "Views in Theology," a periodical published in New York. "It is as true of angels and the spirits of just men made perfect, that they are moral agents, and that their powers are the same in kind that are known to originate sin, as it is of us; as clear that if God 'should begin and pursue any method of providence and government' over them, 'the causes which originate sin would still exist in kind, under his providence,' as it is, that they would among men; and 'since under any system of providence, the condition of his creatures must be constantly changing;' as clear, therefore—if the powers of moral agency alone be considered—'that among these fluctuations, there may arise conjunctures under any providence, in which temptations will rise and prevail to the overthrow of some of those creatures,' as it is that they may, under any providence, over such beings as ourselves.

"On the principles, then, on which his reasoning proceeds, we not only have no certainty of the continued obedience of holy, angelic, and redeemed spirits, but have an absolute probability of their universally yielding to rebellion at some period of their existence, notwithstanding every species and degree of preventing influence that God can exert over them!"

To these, we will add the following from Dr. Griffin: "If God could not have prevented sin in all worlds and ages, he cannot prevent sin in any world or age, or in any creature at any time, except by preventing the particular occasion and temptation. If God could not have prevented sin in the universe, he cannot prevent believers from fatally falling; he cannot prevent Gabriel and Paul from sinking at once into devils, and heaven from turning into a hell. And were he to create new races to fill the vacant seats, they might turn to devils as fast as he created them, in spite of any thing that he could do short of destroying their moral agency. He is liable to be defeated in all his designs, and to be as miserable as he is benevolent. This is infinitely the gloomiest idea that was ever thrown upon the world. It is gloomier than hell itself. For this involves only the destruction of a part, but that involves the wretchedness of God and his whole creation. And how awfully gloomy as it respects the prospects of individual believers! You have no security that you shall stand an hour. And even if you get to heaven, you have no certainty of remaining there a day. All is doubt and sepulchral gloom. And where is the glory of God? Where the transcendent glory of raising to spiritual life a world dead in trespasses and sins? Where the glory of swaying an undivided sceptre, and doing his whole pleasure 'in the army of heaven and among the inhabitants of the earth?'"—*Griffin on Divine Efficiency*, pp. 180, 181.

The *practical* influence of these assumptions is believed to be no less objectionable than their tendencies to error.

1. In relation to prayer. If we adopt the principle that God has not supreme control over the hearts of all men, how can we with confidence plead the fulfilment of those promises which are to be accomplished by the instrumentality of his creatures? However willing he may be to answer our prayers, there may be found among the various agents to be employed, some Pharaoh, so much more obstinate than the king of Egypt, that no influence which God can employ, will incline him to let his people go— or some Ahithophel, so much more sagacious and influential than the counsellor of Absalom, that the Lord will not be able to "turn his counsel to foolishness," and bring back his own anointed to the throne of Israel.

2. If we believe ourselves so independent of God, that we can successfully resist any moral influence which he can bring to bear upon our minds, how feeble will be the incentives to the exercise of humility!

Tell a carnal, unregenerate man, that though God had physical power to create him, he has not moral power to govern him, and you could not furnish his mind with better aliment for pride and rebellion. Should you, after giving this lesson, press upon him the claims of Jehovah, you might expect to be answered, as Moses was by the proud oppressor of Israel: "Who is the Lord, that I should obey his voice?"

3. The same may be said in regard to submission. Of this, the case just referred to affords an ample illustration. What a miserable reflection it would have been to present to an enslaved Israelite, that he ought to submit cheerfully to his bondage, because it was not in the power of the Lord to prevent it! Men are free agents: in the exercise of that agency, your ancestors *would* settle themselves in Egypt—and in the exercise of the same agency, the Egyptians *would* enslave them! God *knew* that such would be the result, and he would have hindered it if he *could*, but *could not*, without destroying their free agency! "Free moral agents *can* do wrong under every possible influence to prevent it."

4. Such reflections afford as little foundation for gratitude as for submission. Why do we feel grateful to God for those favours which are conferred upon us by the agency of our fellow men, except on the principle that they are only instruments in *his* hand—who, without "offering the least violence to their wills, or taking away the liberty or contingency of second causes," "hath most sovereign dominion

over them, to do by them, for them, and upon them, whatsoever himself pleaseth!" On any other ground, *they* would be worthy of the *principal*, and *he* only of *secondary* praise.

In conclusion, we will observe, (adopting the language of the "Views in Theology," already referred to,) "The great questions involved in this controversy, it is sufficiently apparent from the foregoing discussion, are not of mere ordinary interest, but vitally important; and the decisions that are formed respecting them by the teachers of religion, must exert a momentous influence on the churches and religion of our country. The subjects to which they relate—the attributes of God, the reality and nature of his government, the doctrines of his word, the nature of the mind, the laws of its agency, the causes that influence it—if any are entitled to that rank, are fundamental: and the problems which it is the object of the controversy to solve, whether God is almighty as a moral and providential ruler as well as creator, or weak and liable to perpetual frustration; whether he is wholly able or wholly unable, to prevent moral beings from sinning; whether he can or cannot determine and foresee the events of their agency, and thence whether his predictions, threatenings and promises are true or false—indisputably involve all that is essential in Christianity; and the scheme which affirms the one is as diverse from that which asserts the other, as light is from darkness, and truth from falsehood." "The question between them, is nothing less than the question—of two wholly dissimilar and contradictory systems, which is it that is the gospel of the grace of God, and which therefore is it that wholly contradicts and subverts the gospel?"

CHAPTER II.

GOD'S COVENANT WITH ADAM, AND OUR RELATION TO HIM AS OUR FEDERAL HEAD—INVOLVING THE DOCTRINE OF IMPUTATION AND ORIGINAL SIN.

ACCORDING to Witsius, "A covenant of God with man is an agreement between God and man, about the method of obtaining consummate happiness, with the addition of a threatening of eternal destruction, with which the despiser of the happiness offered in that way is to be punished." Such a covenant God made with Adam before the fall; and through him with all his posterity—he acting as their federal head and representative. "The first covenant made with man," says our Confession of Faith, "was a covenant of works, wherein life was promised to Adam, and in him, to his posterity, upon condition of perfect and personal obedience"—(as our Catechism adds,) "forbidding him to eat of the tree of knowledge of good and evil upon pain of death." This has been the common sentiment among the reformed churches since the time of Luther and Calvin. It also formed a part of the creed of the early Christian Fathers.

Some of the reasons for this doctrine are the following:

1. The law given to Adam in Gen. ii. 16, 17, contained all the essential properties of a covenant; viz. parties, a condition, a penalty, and an implied promise. It is not essential to a covenant that the parties should be equal—nor was it necessary in the present case, that Adam should give a formal consent to the terms proposed; because they were binding upon him as a creature of God, independent of his consent. But inasmuch as he was created in the image of God, and had his law written in his heart, there was undoubtedly a cordial assent to the proposed condition.

2. That transaction is referred to by the prophet Hosea, under the name of a covenant. "But they like men [Heb. like Adam,] have transgressed the covenant." Hosea vi. 7. Upon this passage Henry remarks, "Herein they trod in the steps of our first parents; they, *like* Adam, have transgressed the covenant; (so it might very well be read;) as he transgressed the covenant of innocency, so they transgressed the covenant of grace; so treacherously, so foolishly; *there* in paradise, he violated his engagements to God; and there in Canaan, another paradise, they violated their engagements. And by their *treacherous dealing* they, like Adam, have ruined themselves and theirs." This text has no definite sense, unless it refers to Adam.

3. Christ is said to have been given "for a covenant of the people;" (Isa. xlii. 6,) and since a parallel

is drawn by the apostles between Christ and Adam, the latter being called the first, and the former the second Adam, the analogy requires us to regard the first Adam as a party to a covenant.

The representative character of Adam may be proved by the following considerations. All the dispensations of Jehovah concerning Adam before the fall, respected his posterity as well as himself; such as dominion over the creatures, liberty to eat of the productions of the earth, the law of marriage, &c. When God made this covenant with Adam, it does not appear that Eve was yet formed—and yet it is manifest from her reply to the tempter, (Gen. iii. 2, 3,) that she considered herself as included in the transaction. Again; it is said (Gen. v. 2,) that when God created man male and female, he called *their* name Adam; which indicates that the woman was included *federally* in the man. Further; the consequences of Adam's transgression affected his posterity as well as himself. Gen. iii. 16, 19; Rom. v. 12; 1 Cor. xv. 22. The apostle also draws a paralled between Christ and Adam; in which he describes Christ as the representative of his spiritual seed, as Adam was of his natural seed. Rom. v. 12, 19; 1 Cor. xv. 22. But how did Christ represent his seed except in the covenant of grace? Adam, therefore, must have represented his in the covenant of works.

That covenant made with Adam, and through him with his posterity, involves the doctrines of imputation and original sin. Destroy that and you destroy these—they must stand or fall together. And as they are both based upon the same covenant, so they are closely connected with each other. "So far as I know," says President Edwards, "most of those who hold one of these have maintained the other; and most of those who have opposed one have opposed the other. And it may perhaps appear in our future consideration of the subject, that they are closely connected, and that the arguments which prove the one, establish the other, and that there are no more difficulties attending the allowing of one than the other."

Upon these points the Confession of Faith teaches, that our first parents "being the root of all mankind; the guilt of this sin [eating the forbidden fruit] was imputed, and the same death in sin and corrupted nature conveyed to all their prosperity, descending from them by ordinary generation"—and that "from this original corruption, whereby we are utterly indisposed, disabled, and made opposite to all good, and wholly inclined to all evil, do proceed all actual transgressions." The phrase "root of all mankind," it is evident from the proof-texts, refers not merely to natural relation, but also to covenant headship; the latter being the principal foundation upon which the guilt of Adam's first sin is imputed to us; while the former is the *channel* through which our corrupted nature is conveyed. "Original sin is conveyed from our first parents unto their posterity by natural generation, so as all that proceed from them in that way, are conceived and born in sin."—*Larger Catechism.* Imputation regards us as being responsible in law, for what Adam did as our representative —and as a punishment for his sin, our original righteousness was lost, and we are born with a corrupt disposition. That is what is meant by original sin.

As President Edwards is often referred to as a standard author on these points we will quote a few sentences from his work on original sin. "By *original sin*, says he, as the phrase has been most commonly used by divines, is meant *the innate sinful depravity of the heart*. But yet when the doctrine of original sin is spoken of, it is vulgarly understood in that latitude, as to include not only *the depravity of nature*, but the *imputation of Adam's first sin;* or, in other words, the *liableness* or *exposedness* of Adam's posterity in the *divine judgment*, to partake of the *punishment* of that sin."

By the imputation of Adam's sin then, according to President Edwards, is meant liability to punishment on account of his sin—and by original sin, the inherent depravity of our nature. This we believe is in exact accordance with our standards, as they are understood by our most approved commentators.

Dr. Hodge, in his commentary on the Romans, observes, "This doctrine [of imputation] does not include the idea of a mysterious identity of Adam and his race; nor that of a transfer of the moral turpitude of his sin to his descendants. It does not teach that his offence was personally or properly the sin of all men, or that his act was, in any mysterious sense, the act of his posterity." "The sin of Adam, therefore, is no ground to us of remorse." "This doctrine merely teaches that *in virtue of the union representative and natural, between Adam and his posterity, his sin is the ground of their condemnation, that is, of their subjection to penal evils.*" In reference to original sin, he says, "It is not, however, the doctrine of the Scriptures, nor of the reformed churches, nor of our standards, that the corruption of nature of which they speak, is any depravation of the soul, or an essential attribute, or the infusion of any positive evil." "These confessions [of the reformers] teach that *original righteousness was lost,* and BY THAT DEFECT the *tendency to sin* or *corrupt disposition,* or *corruption of nature,* is occasioned. Though they speak of original sin as being first negative, i. e. the *loss of righteousness;* and secondly, positive, or *corruption of nature;* yet by the latter, they state, is to be understood, not the infusion of any thing in *itself sinful,* but an actual *tendency or disposition to evil* resulting from the loss of righteousness." As some of the strongest objections to these doctrines arise either from misunderstanding or misrepresenting them, the only answer which is necessary in many instances, is, to show that the doctrines as held by those who embrace them, are not what the objector supposes. The above quotations will serve to show what are the true doctrines on this subject. Some of the proofs by which they are substantiated, together with such remarks as may occur to us, will be reserved for a subsequent chapter.*

* To any one who desires particular information on these points, we recommend the commentary of the Rev. Dr. Hodge,

We will now state with as much accuracy as we are capable of, what we understand to be the New-school doctrines in reference to this subject. According to the New Theology, there was not, in the proper sense of the word, any covenant made with Adam, but he was merely placed under a law. He was not the federal head or representative of his posterity, but only their natural parent. Though, as his descendants, we feel the effects of his sin, and become sinful ourselves in consequence of it, the doctrine that his sin was imputed to us is unjust and absurd. All sin and holiness consist in acts. To speak of a sinful or holy *nature*, (except in a figurative sense) is, therefore, absurd. When Adam was created, he was neither sinful nor holy, but he acquired a holy character by the performance of holy acts, i. e. by choosing God as his supreme good, and placing his affections upon him. Jesus Christ, though called holy at his birth, was so merely in the sense of dedicated, and not as possessing (morally considered) a holy nature. When we are born we possess no moral character any more than brutes, but we acquire a moral character as soon as we arrive at moral agency, and put forth moral acts. In the sense in which it has been commonly understood, there is no such thing as original sin,

from which we have just quoted. There is no work within my knowledge, which to me is so clear and satisfactory in its statements and reasonings on this subject, and I believe it expresses the views which are generally entertained by those who are denominated the "*Old-school*," or "*Orthodox*" portion of the Presbyterian Church.

there being no other original sin than the first sin a child commits after arriving at moral agency. Children are born with the same nature as Adam possessed at his creation—and the difference between us and him is, that we are born in different *circumstances;* and that the inferior powers of our nature have obtained greater relative strength; from which it universally results as a matter of fact, that our first acts are sinful, instead of being holy, as his were; i. e. we do not choose God as the object of our supreme affection, but the world—and this choice of the world as our chief good is what constitutes human depravity.

Before referring to our authorities, we wish to observe that those who hold either wholly or in part to the above doctrines, have not entirely laid aside the use of the terms covenant, imputation, original sin, &c.—but they employ them in a different sense from that which has been generally attached to them by Calvinistic writers.

Mr. Finney, for example, uses the term *covenant,* in regard to the transaction between God and Adam; and yet he denies that Adam was the federal head of his posterity. His doctrine appears to be that all mankind were placed prospectively under the covenant of works, and were to have a trial or probation, each one for himself, similar to what Adam had; and that from their connection with him as their natural parent, it so happens that they all break the covenant as soon as they arrive at moral agency, and thus become sinners. His language is, "I suppose that *mankind were originally all under a covenant of works*, and that Adam was not so their head or representative, that his obedience or disobedience involved them irresistibly in sin and condemnation, irrespective of their own acts."—*Lectures to Professing Christians*, p. 286. Take these words in connection with what precedes, and their import will be more obvious. "It has been supposed by many," says he, "that there was a *covenant* made with Adam such as this, that if he continued to obey the law for a limited period, all his posterity should be confirmed in holiness and happiness for ever. What the reason is for this belief I am unable to ascertain: I am not aware that the doctrine is taught in the Bible." Here he alludes in direct terms to the common doctrine, and expresses his dissent from it. But what does he hold? "Adam," says he, "was the *natural head* of the human race, and his sin has involved them in its consequences; but not on the principle that his sin is *literally* accounted their sin." [*Quære:* Who does maintain this opinion?] "The truth," he adds, "is simply this: that from the relation in which he stood as their *natural head*, as a matter of fact, his sin has resulted in the sin and ruin of his posterity." Then follows what we first quoted. Thus it appears that though he employs the terms covenant of works, he rejects the doctrine which is generally entertained by those who use them. He intends one thing by them, and they another.

Mr. Barnes, in the seventh edition of his Notes on the Romans, (p. 128,) uses the word *impute*, in reference to the guilt of Adam's first sin; though by a comparison between his remarks here, and some which are found in other parts of the book, it is evident he attaches a different meaning to the word, from what is common among Calvinistic writers. He says, (p. 95,) "I have examined *all* the passages," where the word occurs in the Old Testament, "and as the result of my examination, have come to the conclusion that there is not *one* in which the word is used in the sense of *reckoning* or *imputing* to a man that which does not strictly *belong* to him; or of charging on him that which *ought* not to be charged on him as a matter of personal right. The word is never used to denote *imputing* in the sense of *transferring*, or of charging that on one which does not properly belong to him. The same is the case in the New Testament. The word occurs about forty times, and in a similar signification. No doctrine of *transferring*, or of setting over to a man what does not properly belong to him, be it sin or holiness, can be derived, therefore, from this word."

The *transfer of the moral turpitude* of Adam's sin is no part of the doctrine, as held by its advocates—but this is not what Mr. Barnes intends to deny; because he expressly informs us, that by transferring he means "setting over to a man what does not properly belong to him." The word *impute*, then, according to him, is never used in the sense of "setting over to a man what does not properly belong to him"—i. e. what "*ought* not to be charged on him as a matter of *personal* right." Nor is this *doctrine* taught in any of these passages. How different is this from the language of Turretin and Owen, as quoted by Dr. Hodge. "Imputation," says the former, "is either of *something foreign to us*, or of something properly our own. Sometimes that is imputed to us which is personally ours; in which sense God imputes to sinners their transgressions. *Sometimes that is imputed to us which is without us, and not performed by ourselves; thus the righteousness of Christ is said to be imputed to us, and our sins are imputed to him although he has neither sin in himself, nor we righteousness.* Here we speak of the latter kind of imputation, not the former, because we are talking of a sin committed by Adam, and not by us. . . . . . The foundation, therefore, of imputation, is not only the natural connection which exists between us and Adam, since, in that case, all his sins might be imputed to us, but mainly the moral and federal, in virtue of which God entered into covenant with him as our head." Owen says, "*Things which are not our own originally, inherently, may yet be imputed to us, ex justitia, by the rule of righteousness.* And this may be done upon a double relation unto those whose they are. 1. Federal. 2. Natural. *Things done by one may be imputed unto others, propter relationem fœderalem, because of a covenant relation between them. So the sin of Adam was imputed to all his posterity.* And the ground hereof is, that we stood in the same covenant with him who was our head and representative." . . . . "Nothing is intended by the imputation of sin unto any, but the rendering them justly obnoxious unto the punishishment due unto that sin."

Though, therefore, Mr. Barnes uses the word impute, he does not mean with these authors, that Adam's posterity were rendered legally liable to punishment on account of his sin; but only that they are "subject to pain, and death, and depravity, as the *consequence* of his sin;" "*subject to depravity as the consequence;*" i. e. liable to become depraved as soon as they arrive at moral agency, on account of their being descended from Adam, who was "the head of the race;" and who having sinned, "secured as a certain result that all the race will be sinners also;" such being "the organization of the great society of which he was the head and father." "The drunkard," says he, "secures as a result, commonly, that his family will be reduced to beggary, want and woe. A pirate, or a traitor, will whelm not himself only, but his family in ruin. Such is the great law or constitution, on which society is now organized; and we are not to be surprised that the same *principle* occurred in the *primary organization* of human affairs." Is this the sense in which our Confession of Faith uses the word *impute?* I will leave it for the reader to judge.

Professor Fitch of New Haven has not laid aside the phrase *original sin*, though the whole drift of his discourses on the nature of sin is inconsistent with the common doctrine, and was doubtless intended to overthrow it. If it be true, according to him, "that sin, in every form and instance, is reducible to the act of a moral agent, in which he violates a known rule of duty," how can it be possible that there is any such thing as is called by President Edwards, "*the innate sinful depravity of the heart?*" Professor Fitch does not pretend that there is—and yet he would make his readers believe that he holds to original sin, and he tells us in one of his inferences, that "the subject may assist us in making a right explanation of the doctrine." And what is it? "Nothing can in truth be called original sin, but his first moral choice or preference being evil." One can hardly exculpate him from disingenuousness in retaining the terms, after having adopted principles subversive of their clear import; and then employing them in a sense materially different from common and long established usage. He must certainly have known that his definition of original sin is strikingly at variance with that of Calvin; who describes it as "*an hereditary depravity and corruption of our nature, diffused through every part of the soul,* which first makes us obnoxious to the wrath of God, and then produces those works which the Scriptures denominate the works of the flesh."

We have extended these remarks so much beyond what we anticipated, that the quotations we intended to make in proof of our statement concerning the New-school doctrines, must be reserved for another chapter. We will therefore close the present chapter with a few appropriate and forcible observations of Dr. Miller, taken from his Letters to Presbyterians.

After enumerating most of the New-school doctrines which are brought to view in this chapter, and some others which we shall notice hereafter, he says: "If *Pelagian* and *semi-Pelagian* sentiments existed in the *fifth century*, here they are in all their unquestionable and revolting features. More particularly in regard to the denial of *original sin*, and the assertion of the doctrine of *human ability*, *Pelagius* and his followers never went further than some of the advocates of the doctrines above recited. To attempt to persuade us to the contrary, is to suppose that the record of the published language and opinions of those ancient heretics is lost or forgotten. And to assert that these opinions are reconcilable with the Calvinistic system, is to offer a poor compliment to the memory of the most acute, learned and pious divines, that ever adorned the Church of God, from the days of *Augustine* to those of the venerable band of Puritans, who, after bearing a noble testimony against surrounding errors on the other side of the Atlantic, bore the lamp of truth and planted the standard of Christ in this western hemisphere." These observations are not introduced with a view of influencing the reader to receive the statement they contain, on the mere authority of a venerable name; nor of forestalling his judgment with regard to the points under consideration. All that we expect or desire is, that they will influence him to consider the controversy not as consisting (as some profess to believe) in a mere "strife about words," but as involving important and dangerous errors; and will induce him to give such attention to the proofs we are about to exhibit, and to other sources of evidence to which he may have access, as will enable him to ascertain to his entire satisfaction, whether these things are so. If wise and good men now concur with the "most acute, learned and pious divines that ever adorned the Church of God" in former days, in judging these sentiments to be heretical and pernicious; they claim the careful examination of those who attach any importance to religious truth, and desire to enjoy its invaluable and permanent benefits.

CHAPTER III.

THE SUBJECT OF THE PRECEDING CHAPTER CONTINUED, EXHIBITING THE NEW THEOLOGY CONCERNING GOD'S COVENANT WITH ADAM, AS THE FEDERAL HEAD OF HIS POSTERITY, IMPUTATION, ORIGINAL SIN, &C.

OUR statement in the last chapter concerning the New Theology, though embraced under three or four general heads, involves as many other points, which either grow out of the former, or are so connected with them, that our views of the one will materially affect our sentiments concerning the other. Accordingly, in that statement, these several particulars were presented; but they are so involved in each other, it will not be easy in our quotations to keep them entirely distinct. We shall therefore make no formal divisions, but introduce them in such order as we find most convenient.

I will suppose myself in the company of several prominent ministers, to whom a gentleman present by the name of Querist, proposes the following questions:

Querist.—Mr. Barnes, I have recently perused your sermon on the Way of Salvation, and your Notes on the Romans. Am I correct in supposing that you deny that any covenant was made with Adam, as the federal head or representative of his posterity?

Mr. Barnes.—"Nothing is said of a *covenant* with him. No where in the Scriptures is the term *covenant* applied to any transaction with Adam. All that is established here is the simple fact that Adam sinned, and that this made it certain that all his posterity would be sinners. Beyond this, the language of the Apostle does not go; and all else that has been said of this, is the result of mere philosophical speculation."—*Notes on the Romans*, 1st edition, p. 128.

Querist.—Was not Christ the covenant head of his people, and does not the Apostle draw a parallel between Adam and Christ?

Mr. Barnes.—"A comparison is also instituted between Adam and Christ in 1 Cor. xv. 22—25. The reason is, not that Adam was the *representative* or *federal head* of the human race, about which the Apostle says nothing, and which is not even implied, but that he was the first of the race; he was the fountain, the head, the father; and the consequences of that first act, introducing sin into the world, could be seen every where. The words *representative* and *federal head* are never applied to Adam in the Bible. The reason is, that the word *representative* implies an idea which could not have existed in the case—*the consent of those who are represented.* Besides, the Bible does not teach that they acted in him, or by him; or that he acted *for* them. No passage has ever yet been found that stated this doctrine."—*Notes on the Romans*, 1st edition, pp. 120, 121.

Querist.—I perceive that in the later editions of your Notes the above phraseology is considerably changed—have you altered your sentiments?

Mr. Barnes.—"Some expressions in the former editions have been misunderstood; some are now seen to have been ambiguous; a few that have given offence have been changed, because, *without abandoning any principle of doctrine or interpretation*, I could convey my ideas in language more acceptable and less fitted to produce offence."—Advertisement to the fifth edition. "My views have never changed on the subject that I can now recollect."—*Mr. Barnes's Defence* before the Second Presbytery of Philadelphia, in June and July, 1835.

Querist.—Do you then deny the doctrine of *imputation?*

Mr. Barnes.—"That doctrine is nothing but an effort to explain the *manner* of an event which the Apostle did not think it proper to attempt to explain. That doctrine is, in fact, no explanation. It is introducing an additional difficulty. For, to say that I am blameworthy, or ill-deserving, for a sin in which I had no agency, is no *explanation*, but is involving me in an additional difficulty, still more perplexing, to ascertain how such a doctrine can possibly be just."—*Notes on the Romans*, 7th edition, pp. 121, 122. "Christianity does not charge on men crimes of which they are not guilty. It does not say, as I suppose, that the sinner is held to be personally answerable for the transgressions of Adam, or of any other man."—*Sermon on the Way of Salvation.*

Querist.—You cannot be ignorant, sir, that these views are at variance with the sentiments of Calvinistic writers. The 5th chapter of Romans has been universally considered as teaching this doctrine. President Edwards says: "As this place, in general, is very full and plain, so the doctrine of the corruption of nature, derived from Adam, and also the *imputation of his first sin,* are *both* clearly taught in it. The imputation of Adam's one transgression, is, indeed, most directly and frequently asserted. We are here assured that by ONE MAN'S SIN, death passed upon all; all being adjudged to this punishment, as having sinned (so it is implied) in that one man's sin. And it is repeated over and over, that *all are condemned, many are dead, many made sinners, &c., by one man's offence, by the disobedience of* ONE, and *by* ONE *offence.*" . . . . . . "Though the word *impute* is not used with respect to Adam's sin, yet it is said, *all have sinned;* which, respecting infants, can be true only of their sinning by this sin. And it is said, *by his disobedience many were made sinners;* and *judgment* came upon all by *that sin;* and that by this means, *death* (the wages of sin) *passed on all men,* &c., which phrases amount to full and precise explanations of the word *impute;* and, therefore, do more certainly determine the point really insisted on."—*Edwards on Original Sin,* vol. 2, pp. 512, 517.

Mr. Barnes.—"It is not denied that this [my] language varies from the statements which are often made on the subject, and from the opinion which has been entertained by many men. And it is admitted that it does not accord with that used on the same subject in the Confession of Faith, and in other standards of doctrine. The main difference is, that it is difficult to affix any clear and definite meaning to the expression "we sinned *in* him, and fell *with* him." It is manifest, so far as it is capable of interpretation, that it is intended to convey the idea, not that the sin of Adam is *imputed* to us, or set over to our account; but that there was a *personal identity* constituted between Adam and his posterity, so that it was really *our act,* and *ours only,* after all, that is chargeable on us. This was the idea of Edwards. *The notion of* IMPUTING *sin is an invention of modern times;* and it is not, it *is believed,* the doctrine of the Confession of Faith." . . . "Christianity affirms the fact, that, in connection with the sin of Adam, or as a result, all moral agents in this world will sin, and sinning, will die.—Rom. v. 12—19. It does not affirm, however, any thing about the *mode* in which this would be done. There are many ways conceivable, in which that sin might secure the result, as there are many ways in which all similar *facts* may be explained. The drunkard commonly secures, as a result, the fact, that his family will be beggared, illiterate, perhaps profane or intemperate. Both facts are evidently to be explained on the *same principle* as a part of moral government."—*Note to his Sermon on the Way of Salvation.*

Querist.—Are these the views of the other gentlemen present?

Mr. Duffield.—" If by [the union of representation] is meant nothing more than that Adam did not act exclusively for himself; but that his conduct was to determine the character and conduct of those that should come after him, we will not object. But if it is meant to designate *any positive procedure of God*, in which he made Adam to stand, and required him to act, as the substitute of the persons of his offspring, numerically considered, and by name, head for head, so that they might be held, as in commercial transactions, personally liable for this sin, as being guilty copartners with him in it, we certainly may require other and better proof than what is commonly submitted."—*Duffield on Regeneration*, p. 391.

Querist.—I know of no one who holds the doctrine precisely as you have stated it—but let me inquire whether you believe there existed any *legal* union between Adam and his posterity on account of his being their covenant head; and, that the guilt of his first sin was imputed to them, or set over in law to their account, so that they were thereby subjected to *penal* evils?

Mr. Duffield.—"When it is said, in the second commandment, that God visits the iniquities of the fathers upon the children, unto the third and fourth generations," will it be contended that this is because the former stood as the *representatives* of the latter, acting *legally*, in their name, and for them? We presume not. And yet stronger language cannot be employed to denote the results which flow from Adam's sin, by virtue of our connection with him. Why, then, must we suppose that there is a principle in the one case different from that in the other? And that what seems to flow out of the *natural* relation between parent and children, and to be the *natural* consequence of such relation, must be attributed to a *legal union* or *moral identity* between Adam and his offspring?"—*Duffield on Regeneration*, p. 392.

Querist.—According to this view, what becomes of the old doctrine of original sin, as consisting in the corruption or depravity of our nature? The doctrines of imputation and a *corrupt nature* have been regarded as so closely connected, that the denial of the former involved the rejection of the latter—and the same proofs which have been relied upon to establish the one, have generally been adduced to defend the other. Thus, President Edwards, in the passage already referred to, says: "And the doctrine of original *depravity* is also here taught, [i. e. in Rom. v. 12—21,] where the Apostle says, *by one man sin entered into the world;* having a plain respect (as hath been shown) to that *universal corruption and wickedness,* as well as guilt, which he had before largely treated of." Is original sin to be given up; or so modified as to become an entirely different doctrine?

Dr. Beecher.—" The Reformers with one accord, taught that the sin of Adam was imputed to all his posterity, and that a *corrupt nature descends from him to every one of his posterity,* in consequence of which infants are unholy, unfit for heaven, and justly exposed to future punishment. Their opinion seems to have been, that the very substance or essence of the soul was depraved, and that the moral contamination extended alike to all its powers and faculties, insomuch that sin became a property of every man's nature, and was propagated as really as flesh and blood." . . *" Our Puritan fathers adhered to the doctrine of original sin,* as consisting in the imputation of Adam's sin, and in a *hereditary depravity;* and this continued to be the received doctrine of the churches of New England until after the time of Edwards. He adopted the views of the Reformers on the subject of original sin, as consisting in the imputation of Adam's sin, and a *depraved nature, transmitted by descent.* But after him this mode of stating the subject was gradually changed, until long since, the prevailing doctrine in New England has been, that *men are not guilty of Adam's sin,* and that *depravity* is not of the substance of the soul, nor an inherent or physical quality, but is *wholly volun-*

tary, and *consists in a transgression of the law, in such circumstances as constitute accountability* and desert of punishment."—Dr. Beecher's Controversy with the editor of the *Christian Examiner* in the *Spirit of the Pilgrims*, in 1828, as quoted in the *Biblical Repertory*.*

Querist.—Am I to understand by these remarks, that the doctrine of a *sinful or corrupt nature* has been abandoned?

Dr. Beecher.—"Neither a holy nor a depraved nature is possible without understanding, conscience, and choice. To say of an accountable creature, that he is depraved by nature, is only to say that, rendered capable by his Maker of obedience, he disobeys from the commencement of his accountability." . . . . "A depraved nature can no more exist without voluntary agency and accountability, than a material nature can exist without solidity and extension." . . . . . "If, therefore, man is depraved by nature, it is a voluntary and accountable nature which is depraved, exercised in disobedience to the law of God." . . . . "Native depravity, then, is a state of the affections in a voluntary accountable creature, at variance with divine requirement, from the beginning

---

* Since writing this chapter, I have seen the number of the Spirit of the Pilgrims, in which the above is found, with Dr. Beecher's own signature. In his "Views in Theology," he appears to speak a different language—language not easily reconciled with the above quotation. But as he does not profess to have changed his sentiments, the preceding must be regarded as expressing his opinions.

of accountability."—*Sermon on the Native Character of Man.*

Mr. Finney.—"All depravity [is] *voluntary*—consisting in voluntary transgression. [It is] the sinner's own act. Something of his own creation. That over which he has a perfect control, and for which he is entirely responsible. O! the darkness and confusion, and utter nonsense of that view of depravity which exhibits it, as something lying back, and the cause of all actual transgression."—*Sermons on Important Subjects,* p. 139.

Querist.—Does all sin, then, consist in *acts?*

Professor Fitch.—"Sin, in every form and instance, is reducible to the *act* of a moral agent, in which he violates a known rule of duty."—*Discourses on the Nature of Sin.*

Querist.—By parity of reasoning, all holiness must likewise consist in acts.

Mr. Finney.—"All holiness in God, angels, or men, must be *voluntary*, or it is not holiness.".... "When Adam was first created, and awoke into being, before he had obeyed or disobeyed his Maker, he could have had no moral character at all; he had exercised no affections, no desires, nor put forth any *actions*. In this state he was a complete moral agent; and in this respect in the image of his Maker: but as yet he could have had no moral character; for moral character cannot be a subject of creation, but attaches to voluntary *actions*."—*Sermons on Important Subjects,* pp. 7, 10, 11.

Querist.—If these views are correct, what must be

said concerning infants? Are they neither sinful nor holy?

Mr. Duffield.—"It is a question alike pertinent and important, whether in the incipient period of infancy and childhood there *can* be any *moral character* whatever possessed. Moral character is character acquired by acts of a moral nature. Moral acts are those acts which are contemplated by the law, prescribing the rule of human conduct." . . . "It is obvious that in infancy and incipient childhood, when none of the actions are deliberate, or the result of motive, operating in connection with the knowledge of law, and of the great end of all human actions, no moral *character* can appropriately be predicated." . . "Properly speaking, therefore, we can predicate of it neither sin nor holiness, personally considered." —*Duffield on Regeneration*, pp. 377, 378, 379.

Querist.—Was not Jesus Christ *holy* from his birth?

Mr. Duffield.—"Things inanimate have, in scriptural parlance, sometimes been called *holy*, as the inmost chamber of the temple was called the holy of holies; but then it was because of some especial and peculiar relationship which it had to God. He dwelt in it. It was *set apart* as pre-eminently and exclusively appropriate to God. In this sense the yet unconscious human nature of Christ may be denominated *holy*, for it was the habitation of God, and singularly and exclusively appropriate to him, differing in this respect essentially and entirely from that of any of the descendants of Adam."—*Duffield on Regeneration*, p. 353.

Querist.—If infants are not *sinful* before they arrive at moral agency, and have no legal or covenant connection with Adam as their representative, how can you account for their death?

Mr. Duffield.—"There is no manner of necessity, in order to account for the death of infants, to suppose that the sin of Adam became their personal sin, either in respect of its act, or its *ill desert*. Their death eventuates according to that law of dependence, which marks the whole government of God in this world, by virtue of which the consequences of the act of one man terminate ofttimes on the person of another, when there is not the union of representation."—*Duffield on Regeneration*, p. 389.

Professor Goodrich, of New Haven.—"Infants die. The answer has been given a thousand times; brutes die also. But, ... "animals are not subjects of the moral government of God. Neither are infants previous to moral agency; for what has moral government to do with those who are not moral agents?" . . . . . "Animals, and infants previous to moral agency do, therefore, stand on precisely the same ground in reference to this subject. Suffering and death afford no more evidence of sin in the one case than in the other." — *Christian Spectator*, 1829, p. 373—attributed to Professor Goodrich.

Querist.—If infants do not possess a corrupt nature, please to inform me by what process they become sinful—and how it happens that not one of the human family born in the ordinary way has ever escaped this catastrophe.

Professor Goodrich.—"A child enters the world with a variety of appetites and desires, which are generally acknowledged to be neither sinful nor holy. Committed in a state of utter helplessness, to the assiduity of parental fondness, it commences existence, the object of unceasing care, watchfulness, and concession to those around him. Under such circumstances it is that the natural appetites are first developed, and each advancing month brings them new objects of gratification. The obvious consequence is, that *self-indulgence* becomes the master principle in the soul of every child, long before it can understand that this self-indulgence will interfere with the rights or intrench on the happiness of others. Thus, by repetition, is the force of constitutional propensities accumulating a bias towards self-gratification, which becomes incredibly strong before a knowledge of duty or a sense of right and wrong can possibly have entered the mind. That moment—the commencement of moral agency, at length arrives." . . . . . . "Why then is it so necessary to suppose some distinct evil propensity—some fountain of iniquity in the breast of the child previous to moral action?" . . . . . . "But let us look at facts. Angels sinned. Was the cause which led to their first act of rebellion, in itself sinful? Eve was tempted and fell. Was her natural appetite for food, or her desire for knowledge—to which the temptation was addressed—a sinful feeling? And why may not our constitutional propensities now, lead to the same result at the commencement of moral agency, as was actually exhibited in fallen angels and our first parents, even when advanced in holiness?" . . . . "Did not vehement desire produce sin in Adam's first act of transgression? Was there any previous principle of depravity in him? Why then may not strong constitutional desires be followed *now* by a choice of their objects as well as in the case of Adam?"—*Christian Spectator*, 1829, pp. 366, 367, 368.

Mr. Duffield.—The infant "is placed in a rebellious world, subject to the influence of ignorance, with very limited and imperfect experience, and liable to the strong impulses of appetite and passion." . . . . "Instinct, animal sensation, constitutional susceptibilities create an impulse, which not being counteracted by moral considerations or gracious influence, lead the will in a wrong direction and to wrong objects. It was thus that sin was induced in our holy progenitors. No one can plead in Eve an efficient cause of sin resident in her nature (any *prava vis*) or operative power, sinful in itself, anterior to and apart from her own voluntary acts. And if *she* was led into sin, though characteristically holy, and destitute of any *innate propensity* to sin, where is the necessity for supposing that the sins of her progeny are to be referred to such a cause?" . . . . "Temptation alone is sufficient under present circumstances."—*Duffield on Regeneration*, pp. 310, 379, 380.

"Mr. Finney.—"If it be asked how it happens that children universally adopt the principle of selfishness, unless their nature is sinful, I answer, that they adopt the principle of self-gratification or selfishness, because they possess *human* nature, and come into being under the *peculiar circumstances* in which all the children of Adam are born since the fall; but not because human nature is *itself* sinful. The cause of their becoming sinners is to be found in their nature being what it is, and surrounded by the *peculiar circumstances of temptation* to which they are exposed in a world of sinners." .... "Adam was created in the perfection of *manhood*, certainly not with a sinful *nature*, and yet an appeal to his innocent, constitutional appetites led him into sin. If *adult* Adam, without a sinful nature, and after a season of obedience and perfect holiness, was led to change his mind by an appeal to his innocent, constitutional propensities, how can the fact that *infants* possessing the *same nature with Adam*, and surrounded by circumstances of still greater temptation, universally fall into sin, prove that their *nature is itself* sinful? Is such an inference called for? Is it legitimate? What! holy and adult Adam is led, by an appeal to his innocent constitution, to adopt the principle of selfishness, and no suspicion is or can be entertained, that he had a sinful nature; but if *little children* under circumstances of temptation, aggravated by the fall, are led into sin, we are to believe that *their nature* is sinful! This is wonderful philosophy!"—*Sermons on Important Subjects*, p. 157.

Dr. Taylor.—"If no being can sin without a constitutional propensity to sin, how came Adam to sin?

If one being, as Adam, can sin, and did in fact sin without such a propensity to sin, why may not others?"—*Spirit of the Pilgrims*, vol. 6, p. 13, as quoted by Dow.

Querist.—Do you accord, Dr. Taylor, with the sentiment just expressed by Mr. Finney, that "*infants possess the same nature with Adam*" at his creation?

Dr. Taylor.—"Mankind come into the world with the same nature in *kind* as that with which Adam was created."—*Ibid.* vol. 6, p. 5.

Querist.—What influence then has the fall exerted on the posterity of Adam?

Dr. Taylor.—"I answer, that it may have been to change their nature, not in *kind*, but degree."—*Ibid.* vol. 6. p. 12.

Querist.—On the supposition that the nature of Adam and that of his posterity were alike in kind, why did not he sin as soon as he commenced his moral existence?

Dr. Taylor.—"I answer, that the reason may have been, that his *nature differed*, not in *kind*, but in *degree* from that of his posterity."—*Ibid.*

Querist.—On this principle, in what respect did the human nature of Christ differ from that of other children?—and if he possessed in his human nature, what other children possess, why did he not exhibit the same moral character?

Dr. Taylor.—"I might answer as before, that his human *nature may* have differed from that of other children not in kind, but *degree*."—*Ibid.*

We have given the preceding quotations at considerable length, that those readers who may not have attended to the controversy, may perceive from their own statements, its various bearings and tendencies; and how far those have gone who have been bold enough to follow out their principles to their legitimate and full results. We do not attribute to all whose names we have introduced, every sentiment which has been advanced by some of them—but it cannot fail, we think, to strike the mind of the reader that there is such an affinity between the several parts of the series, that the man who adopts one of the doctrines in this category, will be in great danger of ultimately embracing the whole. They all belong to the same system; and ought therefore to be introduced in stating the distinguishing features of the New Theology; though many who adhere to the system in part, do not go to the *ne plus ultra* of the scheme, as it is here exhibited.

CHAPTER IV.

REMARKS ON IMPUTATION, ORIGINAL SIN, &C., WITH REFERENCE TO THE VIEWS PRESENTED IN THE PRECEDING CHAPTER.

THE controversy respecting our connection with Adam, and the influence produced upon us by the fall, commenced early in the fifth century, when Pelagius, a British monk, published opinions at variance with the common doctrines of the church. He and his followers entertained substantially the same views which have been exhibited in the preceding chapter; though they adopted a method somewhat different to account for the commission of sin by little children, and went farther in their views concerning the influence of Adam's sin upon his descendants. They maintained that "the sin of Adam injured himself alone, and did not affect his posterity;" and that we sin only by "imitation." But their sentiments concerning the nature of sin, original sin, and imputation, were the same with those which distinguish the New Theology.

Concerning the first, Pelagius says, "And here, in my opinion, the first inquiry ought to be, *What is sin?* Is it a substance, or is it a mere name devoid of substance; not a thing, not an existence, not a body, nor any thing else (which has a separate existence) but an *act;* and if this is its nature, as I believe it is, how could that which is devoid of substance debilitate or change human nature?" . . . . . "Every thing, good or evil, praiseworthy or censurable, which we possess, did not originate with us, *but is done by us;* for we are born capable both of good and evil, but not in possession of these qualities; for in our birth we are equally destitute of virtue and vice; and previously to moral agency, there is nothing in man but that which God created in him."— *Biblical Repertory*.

This question concerning the nature of sin was regarded as decisive concerning the other two; and it was introduced by Pelagius with that view. Says he, "It is disputed concerning this, whether our *nature is debilitated and deteriorated by sin.* And here, in my opinion, the first inquiry ought to be, *what is sin?*" &c. So it is regarded at the present time. Says Mr. Finney, "In order to admit the sinfulness of *nature*, we must believe sin to consist in the substance of the constitution, instead of voluntary *action,* which is a thing impossible."—*Sermons on Important Subjects*, p. 158.

Mr. Duffield, after stating several things which he supposes may be meant by the phrase *original sin*, gives as the views of the Westminster divines, that it denotes "something which has the power to originate sin, and which is necessarily involved in our very being, from the first moment of its origination." This he intimates was intended by the expression in our Catechism, "the corruption of our whole nature." He then says, (after some preliminaries) "It is strange that ever it should have been made a question, whether sin may be predicated of being or simple existence, since sin is undeniably an *act* of a *moral* character, and therefore *can* only be committed by one who is possessed of moral powers, i. e. one who is capable of acting according as the law requires or prohibits." . . . . . "Holiness, or sin which is its opposite, has a direct and immediate reference to those voluntary *acts* and exercises, which the law is designed to secure or prevent." . . . . . "How very absurd, therefore, is it to predicate sin of that which does not fall under cognizance of law at all!"

Though he uses the phrase "being or simple existence," as that concerning which it is absurd to predicate sin, he refers unquestionably to the expression in the Catechism which he had just quoted, and upon which he was remarking, viz. "the corruption of our whole nature." It is absurd, therefore, according to him, to speak of our having a corrupt nature, since, as he maintains, all sin consists in voluntary *acts* of a moral agent, in violation of a known law. Hence the imputation of Adam's first sin to his posterity, and original sin, are rejected as unphilosophical and absurd.

Says Pelagius, "When it is declared that all have sinned in Adam, *it should not be understood of any original sin contracted by their birth*, but of imitation." . . . . "How can a man be considered guilty by God of that sin which he knows not to be his own? for if it is necessary, it is not his own; but if it is his own, it is voluntary; and if voluntary, it can be avoided."

Julian, one of the disciples of Pelagius, says, "Whoever is accused of a crime, the charge is made against his conduct, and not against his birth." . . . "Therefore we conclude that the triune God should be adored as most just; and it has been made to appear most irrefragably, that *the sin of another never can be imputed by him to little children.*" . . . "Hence that is evident which we defend as most reasonable, that no one is born in sin, and that God never judges men to be guilty on account of their birth." . . . . . "Children, inasmuch as they are children, never can be guilty, until they have done something by their own proper will."—*Biblical Repertory.*

How striking is the resemblance between these views and the following remarks of Mr. Barnes: "When Paul," says he, "states a simple *fact*, men often advance a *theory*. . . . A melancholy instance of this we have in the account which the apostle gives, (ch. 5.) about the effect of the sin of Adam. . . . . They have sought for a theory to account for it. And many suppose they have found it in the doctrine that the sin of Adam is *imputed*, or set over by an arbitrary arrangement to beings otherwise innocent, and that they are held to be responsible for a deed committed by a man thousands of years before they were born. This is the *theory;* and men insensibly forget that it is *mere theory.*" . . . . "I understand it, therefore, [Rom. v. 12,] as referring to the fact that men sin *in their own persons, sin in themselves*—as indeed how *can* they *sin* in any other way?"—*Notes on the Romans,* pp. 10, 117.

We admit that this coincidence between the New-school doctrines and Pelagianism, does not afford *certain* proof of their being untrue. It is however a strong *presumptive* evidence, since Pelagianism has been rejected as heretical by every Evangelical Church in Christendom.

Cœlestius, a disciple of Pelagius, is said to have been more zealous and successful in the propagation of these errors than his master. Hence, in early times, they were perhaps associated with *his name*, more than with that of Pelagius. Among other councils who condemned his heresy, was the council of Ephesus, A. D. 431; who "denominated it the *wicked doctrine* of Cœlestius."—*Biblical Repertory.*

In a number of the Confessions of Faith adopted by different churches after the Reformation, Pelagianism is mentioned by name. Thus, in one of the Articles of the Episcopal Church, it is said, "Original sin standeth not in the following of *Adam*, (as the *Pelagians* do vainly talk,) but it is the fault and corruption of the nature of every man, that naturally is engendered of the offspring of *Adam*, whereby man is very far gone from original righteousness, and is of his own nature inclined to evil."

Though in the Westminster Confession, this heresy is not expressly *named*, there can be no doubt that the framers intended to reject and condemn it. Compare the preceding doctrines of Pelagius and his followers with our quotations from the Confession of Faith in chap. iii.; also the following from the Larger Catechism: "The sinfulness of that estate whereinto man fell, consisteth in the guilt of *Adam's* first sin, the want of that righteousness wherein he was created, and the corruption of his nature, whereby he is utterly indisposed, disabled, and made opposite unto all that is spiritually good, and wholly inclined to all evil, and that continually: which is commonly called *original sin*, and from which do proceed all actual transgressions."

We have said that the denial of the doctrine of imputation and original sin, arises in part from the adoption of the theory that all sin consists in acts. Upon this point, therefore, it will be pertinent to make a few remarks.

1. Holiness and sin are predicated of the *heart.* Thus the Bible speaks of an honest and good heart, a broken heart, a clean heart, an evil heart, a hard heart, &c., which convey the idea that there is something in man of a moral character, prior to his *acts*—something which forms the basis from which his good and evil *actions* proceed; and which determines the character of those actions. Hence holiness and sin do not consist wholly in acts, but belong to our nature.

2. We are said to be conceived and born in sin; and if so, we must be sinful *by nature;* for we have not then put forth any moral *acts.*

3. We are declared to be by nature the children of wrath—and if children of wrath by nature, then we must be *by nature, sinners,* for sin alone exposes to wrath. All sin therefore cannot consist in *acts.*

4. Adam was created in the image of God—which according to our standards, consisted in "knowledge, righteousness, and holiness." By the fall this image was lost. In regard to *spiritual* things we became ignorant.—"The natural man discerneth not the things of the Spirit of God," &c. Our moral characters became corrrupt and wicked. In other words, we forfeited our original righteousness and became prone to evil. By regeneration this image is restored. Col. iii. 10: "And have put on the new man which is renewed in *knowledge* after the *image*

of him that created him." Eph. iv. 24: "And that ye put on the new man, which *after God* is created in *righteousness and true holiness.*" These texts are decisive as to what the image of God consisted in, viz. "knowledge, righteousness and true holiness." Yet in this image man was *created;* and of course possessed it before he put forth moral acts. Consequently all holiness and sin do not consist in *acts,* but may be predicated of our nature.

The manner in which this argument has been disposed of, is truly singular. On the principle that all holiness consists in *acts,* it cannot be created. This the advocates of the New Theology admit. Since then, Adam was created in the image of God, a new theory must be devised as to what that image was. In this, however, there is not a perfect agreement. According to Mr. Finney, it consisted in moral agency. "In this state, says he, [i. e. when Adam was first created,] he was a *complete moral agent, and in this respect in the image of his Maker.*"— *Sermons on Important Subjects,* p. 11. Mr. Duffield makes it consist principally in some imaginary resemblance to the Trinity. "There is, however," says he, "one important respect in which this resemblance in man to God may be seen, which, indeed, is generally overlooked, but which we are disposed to think is of *principal* consequence. It is not one person of the Godhead only who is represented as speaking at the formation of man, but the whole three. Jehovah, the ever blessed *Three in One,* said, "Let us make man in our image"—not in the image of any one person, nor of each distinctly, but of all *conjointly*. How admirably are the distinct personality and essential unity of the Godhead represented or *imaged* in man possessing three distinct kinds of life, and yet constituting but one moral being! In him are united the *vegetable,* the *animal,* and the *moral* or *spiritual life,* each having and preserving its distinct character, but all combined in one responsible individual."—*Duffield on Regeneration,* p. 143.

What a pity it is that the apostle Paul had not become acquainted with this new theory concerning the nature of sin and holiness! He would not then have committed such a mistake in describing the image of God in which man was created, and to which we are restored by divine grace!

5. It will be perceived by the preceding remarks, that this doctrine involves also a new theory of regeneration. This is not denied—and hence the sentiments which have long prevailed on this subject are rejected, and the notion of *gradual* regeneration by moral *suasion,* is substituted in their place. But as we intend to exhibit this feature of the New Theology more at length in a subsequent chapter, we will not dwell upon it here.

6. This doctrine places those who die in infancy in a most unenviable position. If all sin and holiness consist in the voluntary acts of a moral agent, infants, before arriving at moral agency, have no moral character; but stand in respect to moral government on the same level with brute animals. This is the New-school doctrine. Since, therefore, thousands die

in infancy, where do they go? If they have no moral character, the blessings of the gospel are no more adapted to them, than to the brutes. Hence if they die before they become moral agents, they must either be annihilated, or spend an eternity in some unknown and inconceivable state of existence—neither in heaven nor hell, but possibly between the two—in some *limbus infantum*, similar, perhaps, to that of the papists; yet with this advantage in favour of the latter, that *their* infants, possessing moral character, may be renewed and saved. What a comfortless doctrine must this be to parents, when weeping by the cradle of expiring infancy!*

7. The death of infants affords strong proof of the doctrine of *imputation* and *original sin*. If there is no *legal* connection between us and Adam, if his sin is *not imputed* to us, and we are *not born* with a *corrupt nature*, where is the *justice* of inflicting upon infants who have never committed *actual* transgression, a part of the penalty threatened upon Adam for his disobedience?

8. The doctrine of imputation affords the only evidence we can have, that those dying in infancy are

---

* The manner in which the advocates of the New Theology attempt to relieve themselves from this difficulty, is the following, viz. that the atonement places those who die in infancy in such *circumstances* in the next world, as to result in their becoming holy at the commencement of moral agency. But this supposition has no foundation in Scripture. Christ is never represented as entering our world to prevent men from becoming sinners, but to save those who were sinners already.

saved. If Adam's sin was not imputed to them for their condemnation, how can the righteousness of Christ be imputed to them for their justification? Christ came to "seek and save that which was lost" —"to save sinners"—he saves no others. If, therefore, they were not lost in Adam—if they were not made sinners by his sin—Christ did not come to save them. But he did come to save such. He says, "Suffer little children to come unto me and forbid them not, for of such is the kingdom of heaven." They are therefore sinners—and as they lost their original righteousness through the first Adam, the foundation was laid for their restoration and salvation through the second. On any other principle there would be no hope in their case. But here is ground for consolation. In the language of Dr. Watts,

> "A thousand new-born babes are dead,
> By fatal union to their head:
> But whilst our spirits, filled with awe,
> Behold the terrors of thy law,
> We sing the honours of thy grace,
> That sent to save our ruined race:
> ADAM the second, from the dust
> Raises the ruins of the first."

9. The doctrine of imputation is essential to a correct view of the plan of salvation. As Dr. Hodge has well expressed it: "The denial of this doctrine involves also the denial of the scriptural view of the atonement and justification. It is essential to the scriptural form of these doctrines that the idea of legal substitution should be retained. Christ bore

our sins; our iniquities were laid upon him; which, according to the true meaning of Scripture language, can only signify, that he bore the punishment of those sins; not the same evils indeed either in kind or degree; but still penal, because judicially inflicted for the support of law. . . . . This idea of legal substitution enters also into the scriptural view of justification. In justification, according to Paul's language, God imputes righteousness to the ungodly. This righteousness is not their own; but they are regarded and treated as righteous on account of the obedience of Christ. That is, his righteousness is so laid to their account, or imputed to them, that they are regarded and treated as if it were their own, or as if they had kept the law."—*Hodge on the Romans*, pp. 127, 128.

The connection of imputation with the work of Christ, gives to this doctrine its chief importance. The same principle is applied in the Bible both to Adam and Christ. If, therefore, we deny our *legal* connection with Adam, and the *imputation* of his first sin to his posterity, we must necessarily adopt views concerning the method of salvation by Jesus Christ, materially different from those above given. On the supposition that the principle of representation is inadmissible in the case of Adam, it must be equally so in reference to Christ. If we cannot be condemned in law by the disobedience of the one, we cannot be justified by the obedience of the other. A blow is thus struck at the foundation of our hope;— a blow, which, if it destroys our connection with

Adam, destroys also our connection with Christ, and our title to heaven.

Says Owen, "By some the imputation of the actual apostacy and transgression of Adam, the head of our nature, whereby his sin became the sin of the world, is utterly denied. Hereby both the ground the the apostle proceedeth on, in evincing the necessity of our justification, or our being made righteous by the obedience of another, and all the arguments brought in confirmation of the doctrine of it, in the fifth chapter of his Epistle to the Romans, are evaded and overthrown. Socinus confesseth that place to give great countenance unto the doctrine of justification by the imputation of the righteousness of Christ; and therefore he sets himself to oppose with sundry artifices the imputation of the sin of Adam, unto his natural posterity. For he perceived well enough that upon the admission thereof, the imputation of the righteousness of Christ unto his spiritual seed, would unavoidably follow according unto the tenor of the apostle's discourse." . . . "Some deny the depravation and corruption of our nature, which ensued on our apostacy from God, and the loss of his image. Or if they do not absolutely deny it, yet they so extenuate it, as to render it a matter of no great concern unto us." . . . . "That deformity of soul which came upon us in the loss of the image of God, wherein the beauty and harmony of all our faculties, in all their actings, in order unto their utmost end, did consist; that enmity unto God, even in the mind which ensued thereon; that darkness with which our understandings were clouded, yea, blinded withal; the spiritual death which passed on the whole soul, and total alienation from the life of God; that impotency unto good, that inclination unto evil, that deceitfulness of sin, that power and efficacy of corrupt lusts, which the Scriptures and experience so fully charge on the state of lost nature, are rejected as empty notions, or fables. No wonder if such persons look upon imputed righteousness as the shadow of a dream, who esteem those things which evidence its necessity to be but fond imaginations. And small hope is there to bring such men to value the righteousness of Christ, as imputed to them, who are so unacquainted with their own unrighteousness inherent in them."

10. The Scripture proofs relied upon to establish the doctrine of imputation and original sin, are such as the following. John iii. 3, 6: "Except a man be born again he cannot see the kingdom of God. That which is born of the flesh is flesh, and that which is born of the Spirit is spirit." Here our first or natural birth is contrasted with our second or spiritual birth. If at the first we are unfit for the kingdom of heaven, and are qualified only by the second, then it is clear we are *born sinners*.

Rom. v. 12—21. "As by one man sin entered into the world and death by sin, so death passed upon all men, for that all have sinned, &c. We have already quoted some remarks on this passage from President Edwards, in the last chapter, to which we refer the reader. The quotation commences as follows: "The doctrine of the *corruption of nature*, derived from

Adam, and also the *imputation of his first sin*, are both clearly taught in it," &c. The phrases, "for that, or in whom *all* have *sinned*," "through the offence of *one* many be *dead*," "the judgment was by *one* to *condemnation*," "by *one* man's *offence, death* reigned by *one*," "by *one* man's disobedience many were *made sinners*," and other similar ones, contain so exact a description of the doctrine, that the proof which they furnish would not be more conclusive, if the very words *impute* and *original sin* had been introduced.

Rom. vii. 18—23. "For I know that in me (that is in my flesh) dwelleth no good thing; for to will is present with me; but how to perform that which is good, I find not," &c. This struggle between the old and new man, between indwelling sin and the principle of grace, affords strong evidence of the natural propensity of man to sin.

1 Cor. xv. 22. "For as in Adam all die, even so in Christ shall all be made alive." By simply reversing the order of the passage, its relevancy to our present purpose will be manifest. As all who shall be made alive will enjoy this blessing by virtue of their connection with Christ as their covenant head; so all who die, experience this calamity in consequence of a similar connection with Adam; who "being the root of all mankind, the guilt of [his first sin] was *imputed,* and the same *death in sin, and corrupted nature*, conveyed to all his posterity, descending from him by ordinary generation."

Eph. ii. 3. "And were by nature the children of

wrath, even as others." This has been generally understood, both by ancient and modern commentators, as teaching the doctrine that we are born in a state of sin and condemnation. If we are children of wrath by *nature*, we must have been *born* in that condition; and if born children of *wrath*, we must have been born in *sin*.

In the Old Testament, the following among others may be referred to. Gen. vi. 5: "And God saw that the wickedness of man was great in the earth, and every imagination of the thoughts of his heart was only evil continually." This is descriptive not of one man only, but of the race; and how can this universal corruption be accounted for except on the principle of original sin? Job xiv. 4: "Who can bring a clean thing out of an unclean? not one." If, then, parents are "unclean," if they are universally sinful, children inherit from them the same character. Psal. li. 5: "Behold, I was shapen in iniquity, and in sin did my mother conceive me." This is an express declaration that the Psalmist was conceived in sin; and if it was true of him, it is true of all others. These three passages taken in connection, form a complete syllogism in support of this doctrine. If the first of them is applicable to all mankind, as appears from the similarity of that description, and those given by David and Paul; and if the two latter exhibit the fountain from which the evil imaginations of the heart take their rise, as they appear clearly to indicate; then all men possess a depraved and sinful nature, inherited from their parents.

As the chief object of the present volume is to exhibit the *difference* between the Old and New Theology, we have not thought it expedient to enter largely upon the *proofs* in favour of the former. But what has been adduced is sufficient, we think, to show the truth of the Old system, in opposition to the New, and to serve as a kind of index to a more minute and extensive examination of the subject.

Before closing the chapter we will make a few remarks on the charge of *injustice*, which is brought against the views entertained by the Old-school divines, with regard to this subject. We believe it to be wholly unfounded; but against the opposite theory, it might be made to lie with great force. Does any one pronounce it unjust for a man to be held liable for a debt contracted by one of his ancestors, provided in becoming his heir, that was made one of the *legal* conditions by which he should inherit his estate? But suppose he had no *legal* connection with him at all, but simply the relation of *natural* descent—which, according to the New-school doctrine, is our only connection with Adam—where would be the justice in holding him responsible for the payment of his ancestor's debts? He sustains to him, remember, no *legal* connection, but is held responsible, merely because he is his *descendant*. Is this *just?*—Since then all are obliged to admit that we suffer evils in consequence of Adam's sin, why not adopt the *scripture* doctrine, that being included with him in the *covenant of works*, we became *legally* involved in the ruin brought upon the world by his sin? This covenant or *legal* connection, renders it *just* that we should inherit these calamities—but on any other principle their infliction upon us can not be easily explained, without bearing painfully upon the justice of God's dispensations.

Such is the organization of human governments, that we are usually connected in *law* with those from whom we have *descended*—and there is a fitness and propriety in this arrangement. Hence, unless special provision is made to the contrary, the *natural* descendant becomes the *legal* heir. Such also is the divine economy with regard to man. The appointment of Adam as our federal head was not altogether arbitrary, as it would have been, had he been appointed the federal head of angels—but it was according to the fitness of things. Hence our *natural* relation is made use of as the *medium* of bringing about those results, which have their origin in our *federal* relation. Original sin flows to us through the *channel of natural* descent—and various evils which now flow from parent to child, descend in the same way:—but their *foundation* must be traced back to the *covenant* made with our first father, as the *representative* of his posterity; the guilt of whose first sin being imputed to us, a corrupt and depraved nature and other penal evils follow as the consequence. Is any one disposed to say, I never gave my *consent* to that covenant, and therefore it is unjust to punish me for its violation? We ask in return, whether the individual whose case has been supposed, gave his consent that his ancestor should leave the estate which he has inherited from him, encumbered with debt. And yet, no *sane* man would ever think of calling in question the propriety of his being held responsible. If, however, he had no *legal* connection with that ancestor, his *natural* relation would not be sufficient to bind him. He is his heir, not *merely* because he has *descended* from him, but because the *law of the land* has made him such. The latter and not the former, imposes upon him the liabilities which his ancestor incurred; and though he never gave his consent, he regards it as just and right.

CHAPTER V.

THE SUFFERINGS OF CHRIST AND OUR JUSTIFICATION THROUGH HIM.

THE nature and design of Christ's sufferings are generally described by theological writers of the present day, under the name of Atonement—a term not found in our standards, and but once in the English version of the New Testament. For a considerable time after the Reformation, the mediatorial work of Christ was commonly expressed by the words, *reconciliation, redemption, and satisfaction:* which are the terms employed in our Confession of Faith. This accounts for the fact that the word atonement does not occur in that volume. The mere use of a term is of little consequence, provided the true doctrine is retained. But many have not only laid aside the ancient phraseology, but with it, all that is valuable in the atonement itself. Instead of allowing it to be any proper satisfaction to divine justice, by which a righteous and holy God is propitiated; some affirm that it was designed merely to make an impression on intelligent beings of the righteousness of God, thus opening the way for pardon; and others, that it was intended only to produce a change in the sinner himself by the influence which the scenes of Calvary are calculated to exert on his mind. The latter is the Socinian view, and the second that of the New-school.

It is proper to remark that the view first alluded to, includes the other two. While it regards the atonement as primarily intended to satisfy the justice of God, by answering the demands, and suffering the penalty of his law, it was designed and adapted to make a strong impression both upon the universe and upon the sinner himself. But though the first view includes the others as the greater does the less, these do not include the first, but reject it. By making the atonement consist wholly in the second or third view, there is involved a denial that Christ endured the penalty of the law, or assumed any legal responsibility in our behalf, or made any satisfaction, strictly speaking, to the justice of God—thus giving up what has been regarded by most, if not all evangelical churches since the Reformation, as essential to the atonement.

We wish to observe farther, by way of explanation, that by Christ's enduring the penalty of the law, is not meant that he endured *literally* the same suffering either in *kind* or *duration* which would have been inflicted upon the sinner, if a Saviour had not been provided. In a penalty, some things are *essential*—others *incidental*. It was *essential* to the penalty, that Christ should suffer a violent and ignominious death—but whether he should die by decapitation or by crucifixion, was *incidental*. It was *essential* that he should suffer *for our sins*—but how *long* his sufferings should continue, was *incidental*. If inflicted upon us, they must necessarily be eternal—because sin is an infinite evil, and finite beings cannot endure the punishment which is due to it, except by an eternal duration. But from the infinite dignity of Christ's character, the penal demands of the law could be fully answered by his suffering ever so short a time. A similar remark may be made concerning the remorse of conscience which forms a part of the torments of the wicked. The imputation of our sins to Christ does not involve a transfer of moral character, but only of legal responsibility. In being "made sin for us," Christ did not become personally a sinner—but "was holy and harmless and undefiled." Of course he could have no remorse of conscience, such as a convicted sinner suffers in view of his guilt. But this is merely *incidental*, and depends upon circumstances. Some sinners never appear to feel remorse at all—and no sinner, probably, feels it at all times. What is intended then by Christ's suffering the penalty of the law as our substitute is, that in law he assumed our place, and endured all that was essential in its penal demands—whereby he fully satisfied divine justice, and those who are united to him by faith, are, as an act of *justice to Christ*, but of *free unbounded mercy to them*, "redeemed from the curse of the law," he "being made a curse for them." This doctrine, the Old Theology maintains —the New denies.

The following quotations will exemplify the New-school views. Dr. Beman,* in his "Sermons on the Doctrine of the Atonement," observes: (p. 34,) "The law can have no penal demand except against the offender. With a substitute it has no concern; and though a thousand substitutes should die, the law, in itself considered, and left to its own natural operation, would have the same demand upon the transgressor which it always had. This claim can never be invalidated. This penal demand can never be extinguished." Speaking of those who entertain opposite views, he says, (p. 45,) "They contend that the real penalty of the law was inflicted on Christ; and at the same time acknowledge that the sufferings of Christ were not the same, either in nature or degree, as those sufferings which were threatened against the transgressor. The words of our text [Gal. iii. 13,] are considered by many as furnishing unequivocal testimony to the fact, that Christ

---

* Dr. Beman has not, I believe, published his sentiments on the other points embraced in the New Theology, and therefore I cannot state with *certainty* what they are.

endured the penalty of the law in the room of his people. "Christ hath redeemed us from the curse of the law, being made a curse for us." But it is, in no shape, asserted here, that Christ suffered the penalty of the law. The apostle tells us in what sense he was "made a curse for us." "Cursed is every one that hangeth on a tree." Believers are saved from the curse or penalty of the law by the consideration, that Christ was "made a curse" for them in another and a very different sense. He was "made a curse" inasmuch as he suffered, in order to open the door of hope to man, the pains and ignominy of crucifixion. He hung upon a tree. He died as a malefactor. He died as one accursed." In a note on the next page, with reference to some remarks in a sermon by Dr. Dana, of Londonderry, he observes: "But why is it necessary to support the position, that the curse of the law was inflicted on Christ? If it should be said, the divine veracity was pledged to execute the law—we reply that the divine veracity can find no support in that kind of infliction of the curse which is here supposed. A substantial execution of the law—an endurance of the penalty so far as the nature of the case admitted or required—an infliction of suffering, not upon the transgressor, but upon a surety, when the law had not made the most distant allusion to a surety, certainly has much more the appearance of *evasion* than *execution* of the law." He says, (p. 51,) "As to imputation, we do deny that the sins of men, or of any part of our race, were so transferred to Christ, that they became his sins, or were so reckoned to him, that he sustained their legal responsibilities."* Again, (p. 68,) "There is nothing in the character of Christ's sufferings which can affect or modify the penalty of the law. These sufferings were not legal. They constituted no part of that curse which was threatened against the transgressor."

What then, according to him, was the nature of Christ's sufferings? He says, (p. 35, 36,) "He suffered and died, the just for the unjust;" and those sufferings which he endured as a holy being, were intended, in the case of all those who are finally saved, as a *substitute for the infliction of the penalty of the law*. We say a *substitute for the infliction of the penalty;* for the penalty itself, if it be executed at all, must fall upon the sinner, and upon no one else." Again, (p. 50, 51,) "The atonement was a substitute for the infliction of the penalty of the law—or the sufferings of Christ were a substitute for the punishment of sinners. . . . . . This is vicarious suffering. It is the suffering of Christ in the place of the endless suffering of the sinner." Once more: (p. 64, 65,) "The penalty of the law, strictly speaking, was not inflicted at all; for this penalty, in which was [were] embodied the principles of distributive justice, required the death of the sinner, and did not require the death of Christ. As a substitute for the infliction

---

* The Old Theology does not maintain that our sins "became his sins"—but only that he sustained our legal responsibilities.

of this penalty, God did accept of the sufferings of his Son."

Was there then no satisfaction made to divine justice? Says Dr. Beman, (p. 65,) "The law, or justice, that is, distributive justice, as expressed in the law, has received no satisfaction at all. The whole legal system has been suspended, at least for the present, in order to make way for the operation of one of a different character. In introducing this system of mercy, which involves a suspension of the penal curse, God has required a satisfaction to the principles of general or public justice—a satisfaction which will effectually secure all the good to the universe which is intended to be accomplished by the penalty of the law when inflicted, and, at the same time, prevent all that practical mischief which would result from arresting the hand of punitive justice without the intervention of an atonement." But what does he mean by "*general or public justice?*" He says, (p. 63, 64,) "It has no direct reference to law, but embraces those principles of virtue or benevolence by which we are bound to govern our conduct; and by which God himself governs the universe. It is in this sense that the terms "just" and "righteousness" occur in our text. [Rom. iii. 26.] . . . . This atonement was required, that God might be "just," or righteous, that is, that he might do the thing which was fit and proper, and best and most expedient to be done: and at the same time be at perfect liberty to justify "him which believeth in Jesus."

Let me now inquire, is this what is meant in the

Confession of Faith, where it reads, "The Lord Jesus Christ, by his perfect obedience and sacrifice of himself, which he through the Eternal Spirit once offered up unto God, hath *fully satisfied the justice of his Father?*" We think not. No intimation of this kind is given. The framers of our standards do not appear to have learned that God governs the universe by one kind of justice, viz. by the "principles of virtue or benevolence;" and punishes sinners for rebelling against his government, by another and a different kind, viz. the justice which is "expressed in the law."

Are these two kinds of justice in conflict with each other? or is not God's justice "as expressed in the law," the same kind of justice by which he "governs the universe?" Was not the law founded on the "principles of virtue or benevolence?" Why then could not Jehovah exhibit those principles, by the obedience and sacrifice of Christ in our behalf, *in conformity to the law?* "But when the fulness of the time was come, God sent forth his Son, made of a woman, *made under the law, to redeem them that were under the law*, that we might receive the adoption of sons." Gal. iv. 4, 5. Does this mean that those "under the law," were exposed to the retribution of one kind of justice, and that Christ, who was "made under the law, to redeem them," rendered satisfaction to another and a different kind—to a species of justice unknown to the law, and contrary to it? Does not the law embody those things which "are fit and proper, and best and most expedient to be done?"

If so, why was it necessary to "suspend" it, in order to introduce a code of justice, which "has no direct reference to law," but belongs to a system possessing "a different character?"

These positions, it appears to me, involve the sentiment, that the divine government and law, as the former is now administered, are not in harmony with each other—that the government of God could not be administered according to the "principles of virtue or benevolence," in a manner "fit and proper, and most and best expedient to be done"—without a suspension of "the whole legal system;" or, which is the same thing, a disregard of his law. And if the atonement proceeded on this principle, we cannot perceive why it might not have been dispensed with altogether—for if "the penalty of the law was not inflicted at all," but a system was introduced "which involves a suspension of the legal curse," why might not God as moral Governor, in the exercise of that "virtue or benevolence, by which he governs the universe," and in pursuance of what "was fit and proper, and best and most expedient to be done," have suspended "the whole legal system," and extended pardon to sinners without an atonement?

Dr. Beman assigns three reasons why the atonement was *necessary;* all of which lose their force on the supposition that Christ did not suffer the penalty of the law. He says, "the atonement was necessary as an expression of God's regard for the moral law." But how could it express his regard for the law, provided the law has received no satisfaction at all, "but the whole legal system was suspended in order to make way for the operation of one," which "has no direct reference to law?" Again, he says, "the atonement was necessary in order to evince the divine determination to punish sin, or to execute the penalty of the law." On the principle that Christ acted as our surety, and sustained in our stead those penal evils which were essential to the execution of the threatening contained in the law, we can perceive how "the divine determination to punish sin" was evinced. Not so, however, if we "deny that the sins of men were so reckoned to Christ, that he sustained their legal responsibilities;" and view the atonement as "a system of mercy," in which the "sufferings of Christ were not legal, and constituted no part of that curse which was threatened against the transgressor." This makes the atonenent an entire departure from law, and could therefore never be adduced to show that God has determined to execute its penalty.

The other reason which he assigns for the necessity of the atonement, is liable, on his principles, to the same objection. "The necessity of the atonement, (says he,) will further appear, if we contemplate the relations of this doctrine with the rational universe." . . . . . . "We may naturally suppose, that it was the intention of God, in saving sinners, to make a grand impression upon the universe.". . . . "What effect would the salvation of sinners without an atonement, probably have upon the angels of heaven?" . . . . "This example has taught them to revere the law, and to expect the infliction of the penalty upon every transgressor." ...... "Every angel feels the impression which this public act is calculated to make; and while he dreads, with a new sensation, the penalty, he clings more closely to the precept of the law. But suppose the provisions of this law were entirely set aside, in our world, as would be the case if sinful men were to be saved without an atonement, and, in the estimation of fallen angels, you create war between God and his own eternal law."

Let me now ask, are not "the provisions of the law entirely set aside in our world," according to his scheme? Not, it is true, "by saving sinful men without an atonement;" but by saving them through that *kind* of atonement, which "has no direct reference to law," and "involves a suspension of its legal curse." If the law "has no concern with a substitute;" and if Christ's "sufferings constituted no part of that curse, which was threatened against the transgressor; how can a *view* of his sufferings teach the angels "to revere the law, and to expect the infliction of the penalty upon every transgressor!" Would it not, on the contrary, produce the impression that the law was given up; and its "provisions entirely set aside in our world?" and if this would be the impression upon holy angels, it would be the same upon devils. To use his own language, "in the estimation of fallen angels, you create war between God and his own eternal law." On the principle that Christ suffered the penalty of the law as our substitute, all is plain—but if not, neither man nor angel can tell satisfactorily, how "God can be *just* while he justifies him that believeth; or why, if he can be *just* in bestowing pardon *with an atonement*, he might not be *just* in bestowing it *without* any.

Another work on the atonement, said to have been founded on Dr. Beman's Sermons, has been published in England, by Mr. Jenkyn, and republished in this country, with an introductory recommendation by Dr. Carroll. On these two accounts it may be properly referred to as a specimen of the New Views.* Mr. Jenkyn introduces seven arguments to prove that Christ did not suffer the penalty of the law—but that his sufferings were a substitute for the penalty. According to him, the very idea of an atonement, involves a suspension of the penalty. "An atonement, (says he,) is a measure or an expedient, that is a satisfaction for the *suspension* of the threatened penalty. A suspension or a non-execution of the literal threatening is always implied in an atone-

---

* Concerning Dr. Beman's Discourses, Mr. Jenkyn says:— "This little work is a rich nursery of what Lord Bacon calls 'the seeds of things.' It abounds in living theological principles, each of which, if duly cultivated and reared, would unfold great and ample truths, illustrative of this great doctrine." Concerning Jenkyn's work, Dr. Carroll uses similar language:—"As a treatise, (says he,) on the grand *relations* of the atonement, it is a book which may be emphatically said to contain 'the seeds of things'—the elements of mightier and nobler combinations of thought respecting the sacrifice of Christ, than any modern production." . . . . . . "We believe that its influence on the opinions of theological students and ministers will be great and salutary, beyond computation."

ment." p. 25. "If a man transgress a law, he must, in a just and firm government, be punished. Why? Lest others have a bad opinion of the law and transgress it too. But suppose that this end of the law be secured without punishing the transgressor; suppose that a measure shall be devised by the governor, which shall save the criminal, and yet keep men from having a bad opinion of the law. Why, in such case, all would approve of it, both on the score of justice and on the score of benevolence. For public justice only requires that men should be kept from having such a bad opinion of the law as to break it. If this can be done without inflicting what, in distributive justice, is due to the criminal, public justice is satisfied, because its ends are fully answered. The death of Christ secures this end." p. 140, 1. Again: "The truth of any proposition or declaration consists more in the *spirit* than in the *letter* of it. Truth in a *promise* and truth in a *threatening*, are different, especially in measures of government. Truth in a promise obliges the promiser to perform his word, or else to be regarded as unfaithful and false. But truth in a threatening does not, in the administration of discipline or government, actually oblige to literal execution; it only makes the punishment to be due and admissible. A threatened penalty does not deprive the lawgiver of his sovereign and supra-legal power to dispense with it, if he can secure the ends of it by any other measure." . . . . "This supra-legal prerogative of suspending punishment, God has exercised in many instances, as in the sparing of Nineveh, and I believe in the sparing of our first parents. The identical penalty of the Eden constitution was not literally executed either on man or on Christ. It was not executed on *man*, for then there would have been *no* human race. The first pair would have been destroyed, and mankind would never have come into being. It was not executed on *Christ*. He did no sin; he violated no constitution, and yet he *died*. Surely no law or constitution under which he was, could legally visit him with a penalty. If it be said that he suffered it for others, let it be remembered that immutable verity as much requires that the penalty should be inflicted on the *literal* sinner *only*, as that it should be inflicted at all." p. 64, 65.

In addition to the remarks already made on Dr. Beman's views, which will answer equally well for those of Mr. Jenkyn, we wish to notice a sentiment not before alluded to. It is contained in the last paragraph quoted from Jenkyn, and is as follows, viz: that though God is bound to fulfil his promises, he is not bound to execute his threatenings. This distinction is resorted to for the purpose of avoiding the difficulty, that if God does not inflict the penalty of the law either on the sinner or upon Christ as his substitute, his veracity is thereby impeached. We admit that the divine veracity does not require the execution of a *conditional* threatening, as in the case of Nineveh; but no one will pretend that God's *law* threatened punishment for disobedience *conditionally*. The moment the law was violated, the transgressor fell under the curse. And he must either endure it eternally, or be released by having satisfaction paid to divine justice in some other way. "Cursed is every one that continueth not in all things written in the book of the law, to do them." "In the day thou eatest thereof thou shalt *surely* die." Accordingly, as soon as Adam transgressed he began to feel the curse. He lost God's image and favour—he became *spiritually dead*—and he would have suffered temporal and eternal death, had they not been averted by the interposition of a substitute.* The penalty of the law must be substantially executed.

> "Die he or justice must, unless for him,
> Some other able and as willing, pay
> The rigid satisfaction—death for death."

If God is not bound to fulfil his threatenings, how can it be proved that the punishment of the wicked will be eternal? Though it is distinctly and frequently asserted in the Bible that such will be the doom of the finally impenitent, yet if God's veracity does not require the execution of this threatening, there is no certainty that it will be inflicted: nay, there is much reason to believe the contrary; because if there is nothing in God's character, or law, which

---

* It is sometimes said that God did not execute his threatening upon Adam, because he did not die a temporal death that very day. But the threatening *began* to be inflicted that very day—and this was all which was intended by it. From the nature of the case, *eternal* death cannot be inflicted in a *day*, because it requires an endless duration. Even in the case of the wicked in hell—it has only *begun* to be inflicted—and yet who doubts that they are suffering the penalty of the law?

requires him to punish sin, we may be sure, that his infinite goodness will lead him to release the sinner from condemnation; and thus, atonement or no atonement, all mankind will be saved. But if the *nature* of God requires him to punish sin, and if when he has threatened to punish it, his *veracity* requires him to execute that threatening; then either Christ endured what was essential in the penalty of the law as our substitute, or our union to him by faith cannot shelter us from its penal demands. Its threatenings still lie against us, and must ere long be inflicted. It is not true, therefore, that "there is no condemnation to them that are in Christ Jesus." He is not "a hiding place from the wind; a covert from the tempest."

Mr. Barnes, in his sermon on the Way of Salvation, and in his Notes on the Romans, gives substantially the same view of the atonement with Dr. Beman and Mr. Jenkyn. But in another production of his, viz: an Introductory Essay to Butler's Analogy, which was first published in the *Christian Spectator*, and afterwards prefixed to a new edition of the Analogy, he presents the subject in a manner still more exceptionable. If I mistake not, it is such a view as any Unitarian in the United States would subscribe to. His language is as follows: "Now, in recurring to the analogy of nature, we have only to ask, whether calamities which are hastening to fall on us, are ever put back by the intervention of another. Are there any cases in which either our own crimes or the manifest judgments of God, are bringing ruin upon us, where that ruin is turned aside by the interposition of others? Now we at once cast our eyes backward to all the helpless and dangerous periods of our being. Did God come forth *directly*, and protect us in the defenceless period of infancy? Who watched over the sleep of the cradle, and guarded us in sickness and helplessness? It was the tenderness of a mother bending over our slumbering childhood, foregoing sleep, and rest, and ease, and hailing toil and care that *we* might be defended. Why then is it strange, that when God thus ushers us into existence through the pain and toil of another, he should convey the blessings of a higher existence by the groans and pangs of a higher Mediator? God gives us knowledge. But does he come forth to teach us by inspiration, or guide us by his own hand to the fountains of wisdom? It is by years of patient toil in others that we possess the elements of science, the principles of morals, the endowments of religion. He gives us food and raiment. Is the Great Parent of benevolence seen clothing us by his own hand, or ministering directly to our wants? Who makes provision for the sons and daughters of feebleness, gaiety, or idleness? Who but the care-worn and anxious father and mother, who toil that their offspring may receive these benefits from their hands? Why then may not the garments of salvation and the manna of life come through a higher Mediator, and be the fruit of severer toil and sufferings? Heaven's highest, richest benefits are thus conveyed to the race through thousands of hands acting as *mediums* between man and God. It is thus through the instrumentality of others, that the great Giver of life breathes health into our bodies, and vigour into our frames. And why should he not reach also the sick and weary *mind*—the soul languishing under a long and wretched disease, by the hand of a Mediator? Why should he not kindle the glow of spiritual health on the wan cheek, and infuse celestial life into our veins, by him who is the great Physician of our souls? The very earth, air, waters, are all channels for conveying blessings to us from God. Why then should the infidel stand back, and all sinners frown, when we claim the same thing in redemption, and affirm that in this great concern, 'there is *one* Mediator between God and men, the man Christ Jesus, who gave himself a ransom for all?'

"But still it may be said, that this is not an *atonement*. We admit it. We maintain only that it vindicates the main principle of atonement, and shows that it is according to a *general law*, that God imparts spiritual blessings to us through a Mediator. What, we ask, is the precise objectionable point in the atonement, if it be not that God aids us in our sins and woes, by the self-denial and sufferings of another? And we ask, whether there is any thing so peculiar in such a system, as to make it intrinsically absurd and incredible? Now we think there is nothing more universal and indisputable than a system of nature like this. God has made the whole animal world tributary to man. And it is by the toil and pain of creation, that our wants are supplied, our appetites gratified, our bodies sustained, our sickness alleviated—that is, the impending evils of labour, famine, or disease, are put away by these substituted toils and privations. By the blood of patriots he gives us the blessings of liberty—that is, by *their* sufferings in our defence we are delivered from the miseries of rapine, murder, or slavery, which might have encompassed our dwellings. The toil of a father is the price by which a son is saved from ignorance, depravity, want, or death. The tears of a mother, and her long watchfulness, save from the perils of infancy, and an early death. Friend aids friend by toil; a parent foregoes rest for a child; and the patriot pours out his blood on the altars of freedom, that *others* may enjoy the blessings of liberty—that is, that others may not be doomed to slavery, want, and death.

"Yet still it may be said, that we have not come, in the analogy, to the precise point of the atonement, in producing *reconciliation* with God by the sufferings of another. We ask then, what is the Scripture account of the effect of the atonement in producing reconciliation? Man is justly exposed to suffering. He is guilty, and it is the righteous purpose of God that the guilty should suffer. God is *so* opposed to him that he will inflict suffering on him, unless by an atonement it is prevented. By the intervention of an atonement, therefore, the Scriptures affirm that such sufferings shall be averted. The man shall be saved from the impending calamity. Sufficient for all the purposes of justice and of just government, has fallen on the substitute, and the sinner may be pardoned and reconciled to God. Now, we affirm that in every instance of the substituted sufferings, or self-denial of the parent, the patriot, or the benefactor, there occurs a state of things so analogous to this, as to show that it is in strict accordance with the just government of God, and to remove all the objections to the peculiarity of the atonement. Over a helpless babe ushered into the world, naked, feeble, speechless, there impend hunger, cold, sickness, sudden death—a mother's watchfulness averts these evils. Over a nation impend revolutions, sword, famine, and the pestilence. The blood of the patriot averts these, and the nation smiles in peace. Look at a single instance: Xerxes poured his millions on the shores of Greece. The vast host darkened all the plains, and stretched towards the capital. In the train there followed weeping, blood, conflagration, and the loss of liberty. Leonidas, almost alone, stood in his path. He fought. Who can calculate the effects of the valour and blood of that single man and his compatriots in averting calamities from Greece, and from other nations struggling in the cause of freedom? Who can tell how much of rapine, of cruelty, and of groans and tears it turned away from that nation?"

It is due to Mr. Barnes to state, that he observes in the words immediately following the above extract, "Now we by no means affirm that this is *all* that is meant by an atonement, as revealed by Christianity." Yet in his subsequent remarks he does not advance a single idea which gives a *higher* view of that great transaction, than is presented above: and in the passage we have quoted, he affirms that the view which he has given, "vindicates the *main principle* of atonement." If his illustrations vindicate the *main principle* of atonement, they must convey a correct idea of what the atonement is. But if the reader is left to obtain his knowledge on this subject from these statements, he would adopt a scheme unworthy the name of atonement. Indeed, Mr. Barnes admits, with reference to the first part of his statement, that it is not an atonement; though at the same time he asserts that the "main principle of atonement" is vindicated by the view which he had presented. But if the *"main principle"* of atonement is exhibited in any part of the above extract, or in the whole taken together, we can see no reason for the necessity of a *divine* Mediator; and should be disposed seriously to inquire whether Socinianism is not all the Christianity that we need?*

* The Christian Examiner, a Unitarian periodical, published at Boston, contains a review of Mr. Barnes's Notes on the Romans, in which the writer observes, "On the atonement, our author's views are far in advance of those of the church to which he belongs. Though he maintains that Christ was in some sense a substitute in the place of sinners, he denies a strictly and fully vicarious atonement, and makes the Saviour's death important chiefly as an illustration of the inherent and essential connection between sin and suffering." With regard to the book, the reviewer says, "While, for the most part, we would advise no additions, were the work re-edited under Unitarian supervision, we should note exceedingly few omissions. Indeed, on many of the standard and Trinitarian proof-texts, Mr. Barnes has candidly indicated the inadequacy of the text to prove the doctrine." . . . . "Sometimes Mr.

We shall give but one more specimen of the New Theology on this subject. It will be taken from a sermon of Dr. Murdock, preached before the students at Andover in 1823. He was at that time a professor in the Andover Theological Seminary.

"In this text [Rom. iii. 25, 26,] Paul declares explicitly, what was the immediate *object* of Christ's atoning sacrifice; that is, what effect it had in the economy of redemption, or how it laid a proper foundation for the pardon and the salvation of sinful men. It was the immediate object of this sacrifice *to declare* the righteousness of God: in other words, to display and vindicate the perfect holiness and uprightness of his character as a moral Governor. This display being made, he can with propriety forgive all that believe in Christ Jesus." . . . . "To enable God righteously to pardon the repenting sinner, the atonement must give the same support to law, or must display as impressively the perfect holiness and justice of God, as the execution of the law on transgressors would. It must be something different from the execution of the law itself; because it is to be a substitute for it, something which renders it safe and proper to suspend the regular course of distributive justice." . . . . "Now such an expedient, the text represents the sacrifice of Christ to be. It is a declaration of the righteousness of God; so that he might be just"—might secure the objects of distribu-

Barnes does not so much as suggest a Trinitarian idea in commenting on texts which have been deemed decidedly and irresistibly Trinitarian in their bearing."

tive justice, as it becomes a righteous moral governor to do—'and yet might justify,' or acquit and exempt from punishment him that believeth in Jesus. It was in the nature of it, an exhibition or proof of the righteousness of God. It did not consist in the execution of the law on any being whatever; for it was a substitute for the execution of it." . . . . "Its immediate influence was not on the character and relations of man as transgressors, nor on the claims of the law upon them. Its direct operation was on the feelings and apprehensions of the beings at large, who are under the moral government of God. In two respects it coincided precisely with a public execution of the law itself: its immediate influence was on the same persons; and that influence was produced in the same way—by means of a public exhibition." . . . "The only difficulty is to understand how this exhibition was a display of the righteousness of God. To solve it, some have resorted to the supposition that the Son of God became our *sponsor*, and satisfied the demands of the law by suffering in our stead. But to this hypothesis there are strong objections. To suppose that Christ was really and truly *our sponsor*, and that he suffered in this character, would involve such a transfer of legal obligations and liabilities and merits, as is inadmissible; and to suppose any thing short of this, will not explain the difficulty. For if, while we call him a sponsor, we deny that he was legally holden or responsible for us, and liable in equity to suffer in our stead, we assign no intelligible reason why his sufferings should avail any thing for our benefit, or display at all the righteousness of God." . . . "We must, therefore, resort to some other solution. And what is more simple, and at the same time satisfactory, than that which is suggested by the text? The atonement was an *exhibition or display;* that is, it was a *symbolical transaction.* It was a transaction in which God and his Son were the actors; and they acted in perfect harmony, though performing different parts in the august drama." . . . . "The object of both, in this affecting tragedy, was to make an impression on the minds of rational beings every where and to the end of time. And the impression to be made was, that God is a holy and righteous God; that while inclined to mercy he cannot forget the demands of justice and the danger to his kingdom from the pardon of the guilty; that he must show his feelings on this subject; and show them so clearly and fully that all his rational creatures shall feel that he honours his law while suspending its operation, as much as he would by the execution of it. But how, it may be asked, are these things expressed or represented by this transaction? The answer is—symbolically. The Son of God came down to our world to do and suffer what he did; not merely for the sake of doing those acts and enduring those sorrows, but for the sake of the impression to be made on the minds of all beholders, by his labouring and suffering in this manner."

The principal difference between these views and those of Dr. Beman and others of the same school, is that he has laid aside the usual orthodox terms, and expressed his sentiments in other language. Perhaps this was *one* reason why such a sensation was produced in the community by the appearance of the sermon. Professor Stuart published two discourses, (if I remember correctly,) with a view to counteract its influence; and Dr. Dana, of Londonderry, preached a sermon (probably for the same end,) before the Convention of Congregational and Presbyterian Ministers of New-Hampshire; which was published by their request. From this sermon we shall give some extracts as expressive of the Old Theology on this subject. His text is in Isa. liii. 4, 5, 6; concerning which he observes:

"JEHOVAH, the just, the benevolent JEHOVAH, *is pleased to bruise him and to put him to grief.* UNPARALLELED MYSTERY! How shall it be explained? One fact, and that alone explains it. He suffered as a *substitute*. He suffered not for himself, but for those whom he came to save. This the prophet unequivocally declares in the text; and declares in such variety and accumulation of language, as is calculated to make the very strongest impression on the mind." . . . . "A moment's reflection may convince us that if any of our sinful race are to be pardoned and saved, an atonement is absolutely *necessary*. God is holy and just; infinitely and immutably holy and just. These attributes imply that he has a perfect and irreconcilable aversion to all sin; and must manifest this aversion to his creatures. But how can this be done if sin be pardoned without an atonement? Would not the great Jehovah in this case, practically deny himself? Would not the lustre of his glorious attributes be awfully eclipsed and tarnished? Further, as the Sovereign of the universe, God has given his intelligent creatures a law. This law, while it requires perfect obedience, must likewise be enforced by penalties. Nor is it enough that these penalties be merely denounced. They must be *executed* on those who incur them by transgression; or on a surety. Otherwise, where is the truth of the Lawgiver? Where is the stability of the law? Where is the dignity of government?" .... "Still further, it is easy to see that satisfaction, if made by a surety, must correspond with the debt due from those in whose behalf it is rendered. Mankind universally owe to their heavenly Sovereign, a debt of perfect, undeviating obedience." .... "We have likewise contracted a debt of punishment. This results from the penal sanction of the law, and is proportionate to the evil of sin. It corresponds with the majesty and glory of the Lawgiver, and with our own obligations to obedience. Now if a surety undertake for us, he must pay our debt in both these regards." .... "As to his *sufferings*, we contend not that the Redeemer endured precisely the same misery, in kind or degree, to which the sinner was exposed, and which he must otherwise have endured. This was neither necessary nor possible. Infinite purity could not know the tortures of remorse. Infinite excellence could not feel the anguish of malignant passions. Nor was it needful that the Saviour, in making atonement for human guilt, should sustain sufferings without end. Such, it is admitted, must have been the punishment of the sinner, had he borne it in his own person. But this necessity results, not directly from the penal sanction of the law, but from the impossibility that a finite transgressor should, within any limited period, render satisfaction for his sins. But the infinite dignity of the Saviour imparted an infinite value and efficacy to his *temporary* sufferings. Indeed it cannot be doubted that he endured as much of that same misery to which the sinner stands exposed, as consisted with the perfect innocence, dignity, and glory of his character. He suffered not only the united assaults of human cruelty and infernal rage, but the far more torturing pains of *divine dereliction.* And inasmuch as the Scripture expressly declares that in redeeming us from the law he was *made a curse for us,* we are constrained to conclude that his sufferings were a substantial execution of the threatening of the law; a real endurance of its penalty, so far as the nature of the case admitted or required.

With reference to Dr. Murdock's* views, Dr. Dana observes: "In the first place, it tends, apparently at least, to subvert the law. It declares that 'the atonement is something different from the execution of the law, and a *substitute* for it;' that 'it did not fulfil the law, or satisfy its demands on transgressors.' In accordance with these views, it declares

---

* Dr. Murdock is not mentioned by name.

that 'the justification of believers is not founded on the principles of law and distributive justice;' and further, that it is a real departure from the regular course of justice; and such a departure from it, as leaves the claims of the law on the persons justified for ever unsatisfied. Without commenting at large on these suggestions so peculiar, and so grating (as I apprehend) to the ears and hearts of most Christians, I will simply set before you the Saviour's own intentions, in his advent and mediation; and these as declared in his own words: 'Think not (says he) that I am come to destroy the law or the prophets. I am not come to destroy, but to fulfil. For verily I say unto you, till heaven and earth pass, one jot or one tittle shall in no wise pass from the law till all be fulfilled.' Surely then his atonement was not 'a *substitute* for the execution of the law.' On the contrary, his obedience and sufferings were a substantial fulfilment of its precept and its penalty; and were designed to procure the justification and salvation of men, not through a 'departure from the regular course of justice;' not by 'leaving the claims of the law for ever unsatisfied;' but in perfect accordance with the immutable and everlasting principles both of law and justice." . . . .

2. "This scheme gives us such views of the divine character, as are equally inexplicable and distressing." . . . . "A Being of spotless innocence, and divine dignity; a Being adored by angels and dear to God; a Being, in short, the most lovely and glorious that the intelligent creation ever saw, is subjected

to sufferings more complicated and severe than were ever before endured in our world; and all this not by way of *substitution;* not by way of *satisfaction for the sins of others;* but of *exhibition* or *display!"*

3. "It is a serious question whether the theory in view does not comprise a *virtual denial* of the *atonement* itself. It leaves us the name; but what does it leave of the reality? An *exhibition* is not an atonement. A *display* is not an atonement. A mere *symbolical transaction* is not an atonement." . . .

"Where, then, let it be asked in the *fourth* place, is the foundation of the believer's hope? It is a notorious fact, that the great body of Christians in every age have embraced the doctrine of the vicarious sufferings and obedience of their Saviour. Pressed with a sense of guilt, they have taken refuge in his atoning blood. Conscious of the imperfection of their best obedience, they have trusted in his righteousness alone. United to their Redeemer by living faith, they have assured themselves of a *personal interest* in his atonement and righteousness. And they have exulted in the thought that this method of salvation met all the demands, and secured all the honours, of the divine law and justice. Shall Christians now be told that this is mere dream and delusion; that no proper satisfaction for their sins has ever been made; that their justification is nothing but an *absolute pardon;* and that even this is a 'departure from the regular course of justice?' Doctrine like this is calculated to appal the believer's heart, and plant thorns in his dying pillow. It is even calculated to send a pang to the bosoms of the blest; to silence those anthems of praise which the redeemed on high are offering 'to Him that loved them and washed them from their sins in his own blood.'"

The Old-school Presbyterian views are likewise expressed in the following language of Dr. Alexander: "The penalty of a holy, violated law, was the only thing which stood in the way. Mere sufferings of any one are of no value, except in relation to some end. The sufferings of Christ could no otherwise open a way of pardon but by removing the penalty of the law; but they could have no tendency to remove the penalty but by his enduring it. Sufferings not required by law and justice must have been unjust sufferings, and never could effect any good. Such exhibition could not have the effect of demonstrating God's hatred of sin, for it was not the punishment of sin; nor could it make the impression on the world, that the Ruler of the universe would hereafter punish sin; for, according to this theory, sin goes unpunished, and dreadful sufferings are inflicted on the innocent, to whom no sin is imputed. This scheme as really subverts the true doctrine of atonement, as that of Socinus; and no reason appears why it was necessary that the person making this exhibition should be a divine person."—*Treatise on Justification.*

The whole controversy concerning the *nature* of the atonement, may be resolved into two questions: 1. Is God bound to punish sin? and 2. Does this necessity arise from the *nature* of God, or from circumstances which lie without him? In other words, do his *holiness* and *justice* require him to manifest his abhorrence to sin by inflicting upon it deserved punishment? or does the necessity for manifesting this abhorrence lie only in "reasons of state," as civilians say—i. e. in the necessity of making a salutary impression upon his moral government?

That the *veracity* of God requires him to execute the threatenings of his law, we have already shown. But why do we find such a law in existence?—a law binding him to punish sin? "The opposition of God's *law* to sin," says Symington, is "just the opposition of his *nature* to sin; his nature, not his will, is the ultimate standard of morality. His determination to punish sin is not *voluntary*, but *necessary*. He does not annex a punishment to sin because he *wills* to do so, but because his *nature* requires it. If the whole of such procedure could be resolved into mere volition, then it is not only supposable that God might not have determined to punish sin, but, which is blasphemous, that he might have determined to reward it. This is not more clearly deducible from the nature of a being of perfect moral excellence, than plainly taught in Scripture: "*He will by no means clear the guilty. The Lord is a jealous God, he will not forgive your transgressions nor your sins. Thou art not a God that hath pleasure in wickedness, neither shall evil dwell with thee. God is angry with the wicked every day. The Lord will take vengeance on his adversaries, and he reserveth wrath for his enemies. Who can stand before his indignation? and *who can abide in the fierceness of his anger? Is God unrighteous who taketh vengeance? Our God is a consuming fire."* (Exod. xxiv. 7; Josh. xxiv. 19; Ps. v. 4; vi. 11; Neh. i. 2, 6; Rom. iii. 5; Heb. xii. 29.) We may confidently appeal to every unprejudiced mind whether such descriptions as these do not fully bear us out in the view we have taken of God's retributive justice. And if this view is correct, sin cannot go unpunished; it cannot be pardoned without a satisfaction; God cannot but take vengeance on iniquity; to do otherwise would be to violate the perfection of his nature. Just he is, and just he ever must be; and there is only one way, that of an atoning sacrifice, by which he can be at once a JUST God and a SAVIOUR."—*Symington on the Atonement.*

If the only reason why God is bound to punish sin arises from the effect to be produced upon the universe, then if he had created no other intelligent beings except man, no atonement would have been necessary—because no moral beings would exist, upon whom to make this impression—and of course he might have forgiven us, irrespective of an atonement, without doing any injury to his government. But, if the necessity of punishing sin lies primarily in his *nature*, an atonement would be as necessary for the redemption of a single sinner, if he had been the only being in the universe, as it was under the circumstances in which this scheme of mercy was devised. And this we believe to be the fact. Otherwise God does not possess *essentially*, that *holiness*, which the Scriptures represent as constituting the glory of his character.

If then the question be asked, Why is God bound to punish sin? the first answer is, because it is *right*—*sin* being opposite to his *nature*—and his *nature* therefore requires him to manifest towards it his abhorrence. Is the question repeated? We reply, it is from a regard to his *law* and *government*. Though the former is the *primary* reason, the latter is of great importance, and must never be forgotten. Taken together they show not only the necessity of an atonement in order to the pardon of sin, but that the atonement must consist in a substantial endurance of the penalty of the law. On any other principle, sin goes unpunished; and we are driven to the conclusion before adverted to, that God is not "glorious in *holiness*"—"a *just* God," who "will by no means clear the guilty."

The following extract from Dr. Bellamy will show how nearly the above views correspond with the sentiments prevalent in New England a hundred years ago: "It was fit, if any intelligent creature should at any time swerve at all from the perfect will of God, that he should for ever lose his favour and fall under his everlasting displeasure, for a thing so infinitely wrong: and in such a case it was fit the Governor of the world should be infinitely displeased and publicly testify his infinite displeasure by a punishment adequate thereto, inflicted on the sinning creature. This would satisfy justice; for justice is satisfied when the thing which is wrong is punished according to its desert. Hence, it was fit, when by a constitution, holy, just, and good, Adam was made a public head, to represent his race, and act not only for himself, but for all his posterity; it was fit, I say, that he and all his race, for his first transgression, should lose the favour, and fall under the everlasting displeasure of the Almighty. It was fit that God should be infinitely displeased at so abominable a thing—and that as Governor of the world, he should publicly bear testimony against it, as an infinite evil, by inflicting the infinite punishment the law threatened; i. e. by damning the whole world. This would have satisfied justice; for justice is satisfied when justice takes place—when the guilty are treated with that severity they ought to be—when sin is punished as being what it is. Now Jesus Christ, the Son of God, has, by his Father's appointment and approbation, assumed our nature—taken the place of a guilty world—and had not only Adam's first transgression, but the iniquities of us all laid upon him, and in our room and stead, hath suffered the wrath of God, the curse of the law, offering up himself a sacrifice to God for the sins of men: and hereby the infinite evil of sin and the righteousness of the law are publicly owned and acknowledged, and the deserved punishment voluntarily submitted unto by man, i. e. by his representative: and thus justice is satisfied; for justice is satisfied when justice takes place; and sin is now treated as being what it is, as much as if God had damned the whole world; and God, as Governor, appears as severe against it. And thus the righteousness of God is declared and manifested, by Christ's being set forth to be a propitiation for sin; and he may now be just and yet justify him that believes in Jesus."—*True Religion Delineated*, pp. 332, 333.

Similar to the views here expressed, were those of the early European divines. "There was no defect in the payment he made. We owed a debt of blood to the law, and his life was offered up as a sacrifice; otherwise the *law* had remained in its full vigour and justice had been unsatisfied. That a divine person hath suffered our punishment, is properly the reason of our redemption." . . . . . "*The blood of Christ shed*, (Matt. xxvi. 28,) poured forth from his veins and offered up to God, in that precise consideration, ratifies the *New Testament*. The sum is, our Saviour by his death *suffered the malediction of the law*, and his divine nature gave a full value to his sufferings." . . . . . "And God, who was infinitely provoked, is infinitely pleased."—*Bates.*

"A surety, sponsor, for us, the Lord Christ was, by his voluntary undertaking out of his rich grace and love, to do, answer, and perform all that is required on our parts, that we may enjoy the benefits of the covenant, the grace and glory prepared, proposed, and promised in it, in the way and manner determined on by divine wisdom. And this may be reduced unto two heads: 1. His answering for our transgressions against the first covenant. 2. His purchase and procurement of the grace of the new. He was made a curse for us, that the blessing of Abraham might come upon us. Gal. iii. 13—15. . . . . That is, *he underwent the punishment* due unto our sins, to make atonement for us, by offering himself a *propitiatory sacrifice for the expiation of our sins.*"—*Owen.*

"Christ hath redeemed us who believe in his name from the terrible curse of the law, and bought us off from that servitude and misery to which it inexorably doomed us, by being himself made a curse for us, and *enduring the penalty* which our sins had deserved."—*Doddridge.*

"I wonder that Jerome and Erasmus should labour and seek for I know not what figure of speech, to show that Christ was not called accursed. Truly in this is placed all our hope: in this the infinite love of God is manifested: in this is placed our salvation, that God properly and without any figure, poured out *all his wrath* on his own Son; caused him to be accursed, that he might receive us into his favour. Finally, without any figure, Christ was made a curse for us, in such a manner that unless he had been truly God, he must have remained under the curse for ever, from which, for our sakes, he emerged. For indeed, if the obedience be figurative and imaginary, so must our hope of glory be."—*Beza*, as quoted by Scott.

These several quotations all proceed on the principle that the necessity of the atonement lay *primarily* in the *nature* of God: that his *justice* must be *appeased* by a true and proper *satisfaction*, before it was possible for him to regard sinners with favour; and that this satisfaction having been made by the vicarious and expiatory sacrifice of Jesus Christ, who "hath given himself for us an offering and a sacrifice to God for a sweet smelling savour," pardon and salvation are freely bestowed upon believing sinners, in perfect harmony with all the divine attributes. With the work which Christ performed, God the Father was infinitely well pleased, and through him he looks with complacency upon all who are united to him by faith. He was well pleased, because Christ performed all that law and justice required—for, as Bellamy observes, "justice is satisfied when justice takes place." "I have finished the work," said Christ, "which thou gavest me to do." And again, just before he expired he said, "It is finished." His work of *active* obedience was finished when he uttered the first; and when he spake the last, his work of *suffering* was also completed. We behold him now as "the *Lamb* of God," sacrificed to propitiate the divine favour; John i. 29: as "the *propitiation* for our sins;" 1 John ii. 2: as a "*sin-offering*" presented to God for a sacrifice or expiation; 2 Cor. v. 21, Gr.: as "a ransom," or redemption-price, to "redeem us from the curse of the law;" Matt. xx. 28; Gal. iii. 13: as "the man, God's fellow;" "on whom was laid the iniquity of us all;" who "bare our sins in his own body on the tree;" Zech. xiii. 7; Isa. liii. 6; 1 Pet. ii. 24: as, in fine, both the offering and the priest, who having "appeared to put away sin by the sacrifice of himself," "offered himself without spot to God," and, "by his own blood, entered into the holy place, having obtained eternal redemption for us;" Heb. ix. 12, 14, 26. How explicit are these passages with regard to the *nature* of Christ's sufferings! If Christ did not offer himself a sacrifice for our sins; if he did not endure substantially the penalty of the law in order to make satisfaction to divine justice in behalf of those who should believe in him, we know not how to interpret the plainest language.

It has been objected that the idea of *punishment* was not involved in the Jewish sacrifices, and hence that those passages which describe Christ's mediatorial work by allusions to those sacrifices, do not teach that his sufferings were *penal*. By a reference to Magee on "Atonement and Sacrifice," it will be seen that the Jews regarded the victims offered in sacrifice as "*bearing the guilt*" of the people; which is the same thing as saying that they bore their *punishment*, because guilt and punishment are correlates of each other. The following remarks of Patrick in his Commentary on Lev. xvi. 21, 22, are to the same effect: "Laying of the hand upon the head of the beast was a rite used in all sorts of sacrifices, whether burnt-offerings, peace-offerings, or sin-offerings." .... "This rite signifies as much as if they had said, whatever we have done amiss, let not us, but this sacrifice be charged with it; that is, let it bear the punishment which we deserve." .... "By putting his hand on the head of the goat and confessing their sins over him (with prayer to God to remit them) they were all charged upon the goat, and the punishment of them transferred from the Israelites unto it." .... "And it appears by the form of all other *sin-offerings*, which were occasionally offered at other times, that he who brought them put off the guilt which he had contracted, from himself, and laid it on the sacrifice which was to die for him." Again; "This [i. e. the goat's bearing upon him all their iniquities] shows more fully still the nature of this sacrifice, in which *all their iniquities*, i. e. the punishment of them was laid, that he might carry them away. For this goat was not capable to bear their sins, but only their punishment; as Christ also did, who knew no sin, and yet was made sin, by having the punishment of our sins laid on him."

So clearly is this doctrine taught, and so adapted is it to remedy the guilt and misery of our fallen condition, that we doubt whether a mind truly enlightened can fail to perceive it, or an awakened conscience be insensible to its value. In view of it, I am disposed to exclaim with grateful emotions, "O Lord, I will praise thee: though thou wast angry with me, thine anger is turned away, and thou comfortest me." "God is in Christ reconciling the world unto himself, not imputing their trespasses unto them." "Whosoever believeth on him shall not be confounded."

> "With joy, with grief, that healing hand I see;
> Alas! how low! how far beneath the skies,
> The skies it formed, and now it bleeds for me—
> But bleeds the balm I want—
> There hangs all human hope; that nail supports
> The falling universe: that gone, we drop;
> Horror receives us, and the dismal wish
> Creation had been smothered in her birth."

CHAPTER VI.

JUSTIFICATION—A CONTINUATION OF THE PRECEDING CHAPTER.

INTIMATELY connected with the doctrine of atonement, is that of justification. The different views, therefore, with regard to the former, which have been exhibited in the last chapter, will give a corresponding complexion to our sentiments concerning the latter. Those who maintain that Christ obeyed the law and suffered its penalty in our stead, and thereby made a true and proper satisfaction to divine justice, believe that his obedience and sufferings, constituting what is usually styled his righteousness, are imputed to the believer for his justification; Christ's righteousness being received by faith as the instrument. Accordingly, justification consists not only in the pardon of sin, or, in other words, in the release of the believing sinner from punishment; but also in the acceptance of his person as righteous in the eye of the law, through the obedience of Christ reckoned or imputed to him; by which he has a title to eternal life.

On the contrary, those who deny that Christ obeyed the law and suffered its penalty as our substitute, deny also the imputation of his righteousness for our justification; and though they retain the word justification, they make it consist in mere *pardon*.* In

---

* "The pardon of sin alone can with no propriety be denominated justification. Pardon and justification are not only

the eye of the law, the believer, according to their views, is not justified at all, and never will be through eternity. Though on the ground of what Christ has done, God is pleased to *forgive* the sinner upon his believing, Christ's righteousness is not reckoned in any sense as his, or set down to his account. He believes, and his *faith*, or *act of believing*, is accounted to him for righteousness; that is, faith is so reckoned to his account, that God *treats* him as if he were righteous.

That the views first given accord with the general sentiments of the church since the Reformation is capable of abundant proof. Though in the time of the Reformers the opponents of the true doctrine did not take the same ground, in every respect, which has been taken since, and which is described in the statement just made concerning the views entertained by the advocates of the New Theology; in one particular they are all agreed, viz: in rejecting the imputation of Christ's righteousness; the adoption or denial of which is the basis of all the other differences that exist on this subject. To this doctrine, therefore, the Reformers clung, as the sheet-anchor of the

---

distinct, but in common cases, utterly incompatible. A culprit tried and condemned may among men be pardoned, but it would be a solecism to say, that such a man was justified."....
"But by the plan of salvation through Christ, there is not only a ground for pardon, but there is rendered to the law a RIGHTEOUSNESS, which lays the foundation for an act of justification. By pardon the sinner is freed from condemnation; by justification he is entitled to the heavenly inheritance."—*Dr. Alexander.*

Christian faith. Justification by faith, through the imputed righteousness of Christ—this was their doctrine. And so important did they regard it, that Luther was accustomed to denominate it, (as is well known,) *articulus stantis vel cadentis ecclesiæ;* the very pillar on which the church rests, a denial of which must result in her ruin. The manner in which his mind was brought to entertain clear views on this subject is highly interesting. "Three days and three nights together he lay upon his bed without meat, drink, or any sleep, like a dead man, (as some do write of him,) labouring in soul and spirit upon a certain place of St. Paul in the third chapter of the Romans, "to declare his righteousness," [or justice,] thinking Christ to be sent for no other end but to show forth God's justice, as an executor of his law; till at length being assured and satisfied by the Lord, touching the right meaning of these words, signifying the justice of God to be executed upon his Son to save us from the stroke thereof, he immediately upon the same, started up from his bed, so confirmed in faith, as nothing afterwards could appal him."—*Life of Luther*, prefixed to his Commentary on the Galatians.

The following extracts from Owen on Justification will show the nature of the controversy soon after the Reformation. "There are two grand parties by whom the doctrine of justification by the imputation of the righteousness of Christ is opposed, namely, the Papists and the Socinians. But they proceed on different principles, and unto different ends. The design of the one is to exalt their own merits; of the other, to destroy the merit of Christ." . . . . . "Those of the Roman church plainly say, that upon the infusion of a habit of grace, with the expulsion of sin and the renovation of our natures thereby, which they call the first justification, we are actually justified before God, by our own works of righteousness." . . . . "They say, 'that this righteousness of works is not absolutely perfect, nor in itself able to justify us in the sight of God, but owes all its worth and dignity unto this purpose unto the merit of Christ.' . . . . . But 'Christ hath only merited the first grace for us, that we therewith, and thereby, may merit life eternal.' . . . . . . Hence 'those other ingredients of confession, absolution, penances, or commutations, aids from saints and angels, especially the blessed Virgin, all warmed by the fire of purgatory, and confidently administered unto persons sick of ignorance, darkness, and sin.'" . . . . . . "The Socinians, who expressly oppose the imputation of the righteousness of Christ, plead for a participation of its effects or benefits only." . . . . . "He [Socinus] supposeth, that if all he did in a way of obedience, was due from himself on his own account, and was only the duty which he owed unto God for himself in his station and circumstances, as a man in this world, it cannot be meritorious for us, nor any way imputed unto us. And in like manner to weaken the doctrine of his satisfaction, and the imputation thereof unto us, he contends that Christ offered as a priest for himself, in that kind of offering which he made on the cross." . . . . . "Hereby he excludes the church from any benefit by the mediation of Christ, but only what consists in his doctrine, example, and the exercise of his power in heaven for our good."

"We grant an inherent righteousness in all that do believe." . . . . "'For the fruit of the Spirit is in all goodness, and righteousness, and truth.' Eph. v. 9. 'Being made free from sin, we became the servants of righteousness,' Rom. vi. 18. And our duty it is to 'follow after righteousness, godliness, faith, love, meekness,' 1 Tim. ii. 22." . . . . "But although this righteousness of believers be on other accounts like the fruit of the vine, that glads the heart of God and man, yet as unto our justification before God, it is like the *wood* of the vine—a pin is not to be taken from it to hang any weight of this cause upon." . . . . "That righteousness which neither answereth the law of God, nor the end of God in our justification by the gospel, is not that whereon we are justified. But such is this inherent righteousness of believers, even of the best of them." . . . . "It is imperfect with respect unto every act and duty of it, whether internal or external. There is iniquity cleaving unto our holy things, and all our 'righteousness are as filthy rags.' Isa. lxiv. 6."

"That which is imputed, is the righteousness of Christ; and briefly I understand hereby, his whole obedience unto God in all that he did and suffered for the church. This I say is imputed unto believers, so as to become their only righteousness before God unto the justification of life." . . . . "The judgment

of the reformed churches herein is known unto all."
. . . . "Especially the Church of England is in her doctrine express as unto the imputation of the righteousness of Christ, both active and passive, as it is usually distinguished. This hath been of late so fully manifested out of her authentic writings, that is, the articles of religion, and books of homilies, and other writings publicly authorized, that it is altogether needless to give any further demonstration of it."
. . . . "The law hath two parts or powers; 1. Its preceptive part. . . . . 2. The sanction on supposition of disobedience, binding the sinner unto punishment." . . . . "The Lord Jesus Christ fulfilled the whole law for us; he did not only undergo the penalty of it due unto our sins, but also yielded that perfect obedience which it did require." . . . . "Christ's fulfilling the law in obedience unto its commands, is no less imputed unto us for our justification, than his undergoing the penalty of it is." . . . . "For why was it necessary, or why would God have it so, that the Lord Christ, as the surety of the covenant, should undergo the curse and penalty of the law, which we had incurred the guilt of, by sin, that we may be justified in his sight? Was it not that the glory and honour of his righteousness, as the author of the law, and the supreme Governor of all mankind thereby, might not be violated in the absolute impunity of the infringers of it? And if it was requisite unto the glory of God, that the penalty of the law should be undergone for us, or suffered by our surety in our stead, because we had sinned; wherefore is it not as

requisite unto the glory of God, that the preceptive part of the law be complied withal for us, inasmuch as obedience thereunto is required of us? And as we are no more able of ourselves to fulfil the law, in a way of obedience, than to undergo the penalty of it, so as that we may be justified thereby; so no reason can be given, why God is not as much concerned in honour and glory, that the preceptive power and part of the law be complied withal by perfect obedience, as that the sanction of it be established by undergoing its penalty." .... "The conscience of a convinced sinner, who presents himself in the presence of God, finds all practically reduced unto this one point, viz: whether he will trust unto his own personal inherent righteousness, or in a full renunciation of it, betake himself unto the grace of God, and the righteousness of Christ alone." .... "The latter is the true and only relief of distressed consciences, of sinners who are weary and heavy laden—that which alone they may oppose unto the sentence of the law, and interpose between God's justice and their souls, wherein they may take shelter from the storms of that wrath which abideth on them that believe not."

These views of Owen accord with the doctrine of our Confession of Faith and with the sentiments of other standard writers. The language of our Confession is as follows: "Those whom God effectually calleth, he also freely justifieth; not by infusing righteousness into them, but by pardoning their sins, and by accounting and accepting their persons as righteous, not for any thing wrought in them, or done by them, but for Christ's sake alone: not by imputing faith itself, the act of believing, or any other evangelical obedience to them, as their righteousness; but by imputing the obedience and satisfaction of Christ unto them, they receiving and resting on him and his righteousness by faith." Says Calvin, "He is said to be *justified in the sight of God*, who in the divine judgment is reputed righteous, and accepted on account of his righteousness." . . . "He must be said, therefore, to be *justified by works*, whose life discovers such purity and holiness as to deserve the character of righteousness before the throne of God; or who, by the integrity of his works, can answer and satisfy the divine judgment. On the other hand, he will be *justified by faith*, who being excluded from the righteousness of works, apprehends by faith the righteousness of Christ, invested in which he appears in the sight of God, not as a sinner, but as a righteous man. Thus we simply explain justification to be an acceptance by which God receives into his favour and esteems us as righteous persons; and we say that it consists in the remission of sins and the imputation of Christ's righteousness.—*Calvin's Institutes*, vol. 2, pp. 203, 204.

These remarks, let it be remembered, refer to our relation to God in point of *law*. "Imputation is never represented as affecting the moral character, but merely the relation of men to God and his law. To impute sin, is to regard and treat as a sinner; and to impute righteousness is to regard and treat as righteous."—*Hodge on the Romans*, pp. 225, 226. Though personally considered, we are sinners, and as such, wholly undeserving, yet when we are united to Christ by faith, his righteousness is so imputed to us, or reckoned in law to our account, that God regards and treats us as righteous—"the righteousness of the law being" considered as "fulfilled in us," because Christ has fulfilled it for us. It is therefore no ground for self-complacency, but of humiliation and gratitude.

With reference to those to whom Christ's righteousness is imputed for their justification, our standards say, "Yet inasmuch as he [Christ] was given by the Father for them, and his obedience and satisfaction accepted in their stead, and both freely, not for any thing in them, their justification is only of free grace; that both the exact justice and rich grace of God might be glorified in the justification of sinners." Thus, according to this view of the doctrine, justice and mercy are harmoniously and sweetly blended. While the sinner is saved without conflicting with the claims of God's law, it is "all to the praise of his glorious grace." We have other quotations to make on this subject, but shall reserve them until we present a few specimens of the New Theology.

Says Mr. Finney, "Gospel justification is not by the imputed righteousness of Christ. Under the gospel, sinners are not justified by having the obedience of Jesus Christ set down to their account, as if he had obeyed the law for them or in their stead. It is not an uncommon mistake to suppose that when sinners are justified under the gospel they are accounted righteous in the eye of the law, by having the obedience or righteousness of Christ imputed to them. I have not time to go into an examination of this subject now. I can only say that this idea is absurd and impossible, for the reason that Jesus Christ was bound to obey the law for himself, and could no more perform works of supererogation, or obey on our account, than any body else."* . . . . "Abraham's faith was imputed to him for righteousness, because it was itself an act of righteousness, and because it worked by love, and therefore produced holiness. Justifying faith is holiness, so far as it goes, and produces holiness of heart and life, and is imputed to the believer as holiness, not instead of holiness."—*Lectures to Professing Christians*, pp. 215, 216.

Mr. Barnes says, "The phrase *righteousness of God* is equivalent to *God's plan of justifying men*"—in regard to which, he observes, "It is not that *his* righteousness becomes *ours*. This is not true; and there is no intelligible sense in which that can be understood. But it is God's plan for *pardoning* sin, and for *treating us* as if we had not committed it."—*Notes on the Romans*, pp. 28, 29. Again, (p. 94,) in reference to the phrase, "Abraham believed God, and it was counted unto him for righteousness," he remarks, "The word 'it' here, evidently refers to the *act*

* This is a *Socinian* objection; and on Socinian *principles* it is valid; but if Christ be *divine*, it has no force.

of believing. *It does not refer to the righteousness of another—of God, or of the Messiah;* but the discussion is solely of the *strong act* of Abraham's faith, which in *some sense* was counted to him for righteousness. In what sense this was, is explained directly after. All that is material to remark here is, that *the act* of Abraham, the strong confidence of his mind in the promises of God, his unwavering assurance that what God had promised he would perform, was reckoned for righteousness. The same thing is more fully expressed, verse 18, 22. When, therefore, it is said that the righteousness of Christ is accounted or imputed to us; when it is said that his merits are transferred and reckoned as ours; whatever may be the truth of the doctrine, it cannot be defended by *this* passage of Scripture. Faith is always an act of the mind." . . . . "*God promises; the man believes; and this is the whole of it.*" It is manifest that Mr. Barnes intended in these passages to deny that we are justified by the imputation of Christ's righteousness; and with regard to the manner in which we *are* justified, he is directly at variance with the Confession of Faith. He teaches that the *act of believing* is imputed for righteousness; and the Confession of Faith declares expressly to the contrary—"not by imputing faith itself, the act of believing, or any other evangelical obedience to them, as their righteousness." The Confession teaches, moreover, that we are justified on principles of law and justice, as well as of grace and mercy—all of them harmoniously meeting together in the cross of Christ. He intimates that legal principles have nothing to do in the matter. "It [Rom. i. 17,] does not touch the question, whether it is by imputed righteousness or not; it does not say that it is on legal principles."—*Notes on the Romans*, p. 28. This sentence, though it does not amount to a positive denial, was designed, we have no doubt, to convey this idea. Similar forms of expression often occur in this volume, where it is evident from the connection, he means to be understood as denying the doctrine.

The New Haven divines appear to entertain the same sentiments; as the following from *the Christian Spectator* will serve to show: "What then is the ground on which the penitent sinner is pardoned? It is not that the sufferings of Christ were of the nature of *punishment;* for being innocent, he had no sins of his own to be punished for; and as he was a distinct being from us, he could not be strictly punished for ours." . . . . "It is not that by his death he satisfied the penal justice of God; for if he did, punishment could not be equitably inflicted on sinners, whether penitent or not. Nor indeed is it that the righteousness of Christ is imputed to those who are pardoned, either as a personal quality, or in such a manner as to be accounted to them as *if* it were theirs. Nothing can be imputed but that which is their own personal attribute or act. Hence, though Dr. B.* does in one

---

* The person referred to here is not Dr. Beman; but if one will turn to *Beman on the Atonement*, p. 51, he will perceive that most of what is here said is more applicable to him than to Dr. Bellamy, whom it is believed the reviewer has treated

place speak of the imputation of Christ's righteousness to believers, he obviously refers not to its transfer, but to the enjoyment of its *consequences;* and he more commonly speaks 'of faith,' a personal quality of the saints, 'as imputed for righteousness.' What then is the ground on which forgiveness is bestowed? It is simply this, that the death of Christ removed the difficulties which would otherwise have eternally barred the exercise of pardoning mercy."—*Christian Spectator*, September, 1830.

How radically different are these sentiments from the doctrines of justification as held by most evangelical churches! If they are scriptural, then multitudes of Christians have mistaken the way of salvation. But if they are erroneous, (as we believe them to be,) then those who embrace them have reason to examine anew the foundation of their hopes for eternity. The two systems can never be made to harmonize with each other. If the one is scriptural, the other must fall; and they involve points which affect so seriously the great and everlasting interests of man, that no one ought to be indifferent with regard to them. Indifference here would be highly criminal.

For the purpose of showing how fully the Old Theology on this subject accords with the general voice of the church since the Reformation, we shall introduce a few additional quotations.

Bates.—"There are but two ways of appearing before the righteous and supreme Judge: 1. In sin-

---

unfairly. See quotations from Dr. Bellamy in subsequent pages.

less obedience. . . . . . Whoever presumes to appear before God's judgment-seat, in his own righteousness, shall be covered with confusion. 2. By the righteousness of Christ. This alone absolves from the guilt of sin, saves from hell, and can endure the trial of God's tribunal. This the apostle prized as his invaluable treasure, (Phil. iii. 9,) in comparison of which *all other things are but dross and dung*, "that I may be found in him, not having mine own righteousness, which is of the law, but that which is through the faith of Christ, the righteousness which is of God by faith." That which he ordained and rewarded in the person of our Redeemer, he cannot but accept. Now *this righteousness is meritoriously imputed to believers.*"—*Harmony of the Divine Attributes*, pp. 298, 299.

Bellamy.—"By *the first covenant*, the constitution with Adam, his perfect obedience through his appointed time of trial, would, by virtue of that constitution or covenant, have entitled us to everlasting life. By the *second covenant*, the perfect righteousness of Christ, the *second Adam*, entitles all true believers to everlasting life, by and according to this new and living way. A perfect righteousness was necessary according to the law of nature, and a perfect righteousness is insisted upon in both covenants. According to the law of nature, it was to be performed *personally;* but according to both covenants, it is appointed to be performed by a *public head.* According to the first covenant we were to have been interested in the righteousness of our public head, by virtue of our union to him as his posterity, for whom he was appointed to act. According to the second covenant, we are interested in the righteousness of Christ, our public head, by virtue of our union to him by faith."—*True Religion Delineated*, pp. 421, 422.

Edwards.—"It is absolutely necessary, that in order to a sinner's being justified, the righteousness of some other should be reckoned to his account; for it is declared that the person justified is looked upon as (in himself) ungodly; but God neither will nor can justify a person without a righteousness; for justification is manifestly a *forensic* term, as the word is used in Scripture, and a judicial thing, or the act of a judge. So that if a person should be justified without a righteousness, the judgment would not be according to truth. The sentence of justification would be a false sentence, unless there be a righteousness performed, that is by the judge properly looked upon as his. To say that God does not justify the sinner without sincere, though an imperfect obedience, does not help the case; for an imperfect righteousness before a judge is no righteousness." . . . . "God doth in the sentence of justification pronounce a sinner perfectly righteous, or else he would need a further justification after he is justified." . . . . "By that [Christ's] righteousness being *imputed* to us, is meant no other than this, that the righteousness of Christ is accepted for us, and admitted instead of that perfect inherent righteousness which ought to be in ourselves. Christ's perfect obedience shall be reckoned to our account, so that we shall have the benefit of it, as though we had performed it ourselves. And so we suppose that a title to eternal life is given us as the reward of this righteousness." . . . . "There is the very same need of Christ's obeying the law in our stead, in order to the reward, as of his suffering the penalty of the law in our stead, in order to our escaping the penalty; and the same reason why one should be acepted on our account, as the other." . . . . . "Faith justifies, or gives an interest in Christ's satisfaction and merits, and a right to the benefits procured thereby, as it thus makes Christ and the believer *one* in the acceptance of the supreme Judge." . . . . "What is *real* in the union between Christ and his people, is the foundation of what is *legal;* that is, it is something really in them, and between them, uniting them, that is the ground of the suitableness of their being accounted as one by the judge." . . . . "God does not give those that believe, an union with or an interest in the Saviour as a *reward* for faith, but only because faith is the soul's *active* uniting with Christ, or is itself the very act of union, *on their part.*"

Concerning the opinion of those who believe justification to be nothing more than pardon, Edwards observes: "Some suppose that nothing more is intended in Scripture by justification than barely the remission of sins. If so, it is very strange, if we consider the nature of the case; for it is most evident, and none will deny, that it is with respect to the rule or *law* of God, we are under, that we are said in Scripture to be either justified or condemned. Now, what is it to justify a person as the subject of a *law* or rule, but to judge him as standing *right* with respect to that rule? To justify a person in a particular case, is to approve of him as standing *right*, as subject to the *law* in that case; and to justify in general, is to pass him in judgment, as standing right in a state correspondent to the law or rule in general; but certainly, in order to a person's being looked on as standing right with respect to the rule in general, or in a state corresponding with the law of God, more is needful than not having the guilt of sin; for whatever that law is, whether a new or an old one, doubtless something positive is needed in order to its being answered. We are no more justified by the voice of the law, or of him that judges according to it, by a mere pardon of sin, than Adam, our first surety, was justified by the law at the first point of his existence, before he had fulfilled the obedience of the law, or had so much as any trial, whether he would fulfil it or no. If Adam had finished his course of perfect obedience, he would have been justified; and certainly his justification would have implied something more than what is merely negative; he would have been approved of, as having fulfilled the righteousness of the law, and accordingly would have been adjudged to the reward of it. So Christ, our second surety, was not justified till he had done the work the Father had appointed him, and kept the Father's commandments through all trials; and then in his resurrection he was justified. When he had been put to death in the flesh, but quickened by the Spirit, 1 Pet. iii. 18, then he that was manifest in the flesh was justified in the Spirit, 1 Tim. iii. 16; but God, when he justified him in raising him from the dead, did not only release him from his humiliation for sin, and acquit him from any further suffering or abasement for it, but admitted him to that eternal and immortal life, and to the beginning of that exaltation that was the reward of what he had done. And, indeed, the justification of a believer is no other than his being admitted to communion in the justification of this Head and Surety of all believers; for as Christ suffered the punishment of sin, not as a private person, but as our Surety; so when, after this suffering, he was raised from the dead, he was therein justified, not as a private person, but as the Surety and Representative of all that should believe in him." . . . . "To suppose that all Christ does is only to make atonement for us by suffering, is to make him our Saviour but in part. It is to rob him of half his glory as a Saviour. For if so, all that he does is to deliver us from hell; he does not purchase heaven for us."—*Discourse on Justification.*

Alexander.—"Some have attempted to evade the doctrine [of the imputation of Christ's righteousness] by alleging, that not the righteousness of Christ but its effects are imputed to us. They who talk thus do not seem to understand what they say. It must be by the imputation of the righteousness that the good effects are derived to us; but the imputation of the effects themselves cannot be. To talk of imputing pardon—of imputing justification—imputing peace,

&c., is to use words without meaning. What we are inquiring after, is the reason why these blessings become ours. It cannot be on account of our own righteousness, which is of the law; it must be on account of the righteousness of Christ. The next question is, how does that righteousness avail to obtain for us pardon and justification and peace with God? The answer is, by imputation; that is, it is set down to our credit. God accepts it on our behalf; yea, he bestows it upon us. If there be any such thing as imputation, it must be of the righteousness of Christ itself, and the benefits connected with salvation flow from this imputation. We conclude, therefore, that the righteousness of Christ can only justify us, by being imputed to us."

In reply to the objection that this doctrine "makes the sinner's justification a matter of justice and not of grace," he says, "All theories which suppose that grace is exercised at the expense of justice, or that in order to the manifestation of grace, law and justice must be suspended, labour under a radical mistake in theology, which cannot but introduce darkness and perplexity into their whole system. Indeed, if law and justice could have been set aside or suspended, there had been no occasion for the plan of redemption. The only reason why sinners could not be saved was, that the law and justice of God stood in the way; but if, by a sovereign act, these obstacles could have been removed, salvation might have been accomplished without an atonement. But though the Scriptures, everywhere, ascribe salvation to GRACE,

FREE GRACE; yet they never teach that this grace requires God to deny himself, as to his attribute of justice; or that law and justice are at all interfered with, or for a moment suspended. On the contrary, the idea is continually kept in view, that grace reigns *through righteousness;* that the propitiation of Christ is necessary, that God may be just and yet the justifier of the ungodly. Redemption is the obtaining deliverance by paying a price; and yet redemption and grace, so far from being inconsistent, are constantly united, as parts of the same glorious plan, according to the Scriptures. 'In whom we have redemption through his blood, the forgiveness of sins, according to the riches of his grace.' (Eph. i. 7.) The only way in which it was possible for grace to be exercised, was by a plan which made provision for the complete satisfaction of law and justice. This was the great problem, to the solution of which no finite wisdom was competent; but which the infinite wisdom of Jehovah has accomplished by the mission and sacrifice of his own dear Son. What is objected, therefore, is a thing essential to the exercise of grace. And the whole appearance of plausibility in the objection arises from not distinguishing between God's dealings with our substitute and with *us.* To him there was no mercy shown; the whole process was in strict execution of law and justice. The last farthing due, so to speak, was exacted of our Surety, when he stood in our place, under the holy and sin-avenging law of God. But this exercise of justice towards him was the very thing which opened the way for superabounding mercy towards us. And this cost at which the sluices of grace were opened, so far from lessening, constitutes its riches and glory."*

We will close our extracts by a few sentences bearing upon the New-school doctrine, that the *act of believing* is imputed for righteousness. They shall be from the pen of Dr. Doddridge, in his note on the phrase, "imputed to him [Abraham] for righteousness;" which is the principal text relied upon to prove the new doctrine. He says, "I think nothing can be easier than to understand how this may be said in full consistence with our being justified by the imputation of the righteousness of Christ, that is, our being treated by God as righteous, for the sake of what he has done and suffered: for though this be the meritorious cause of our acceptance with God, yet faith may be said to be *imputed to us, in order to our being justified*, or becoming righteous: that is, according to the view which I have elsewhere more largely stated, as we are charged as debtors in the book of God's account, what Christ has done in fulfilling all righteousness for us is charged as the grand balance of the account; but that it may appear that we are according to the tenor of the gospel entitled

---

* This extract from Dr. Alexander, and those which have been before given from his pen, are contained in a short and able Treatise on Justification by Faith, written by him for the Presbyterian Tract Society, now the Board of Publication of the Presbyterian Church. This tract, and the other tracts published by that Board, we recommend to the perusal of our readers.

to the benefit of this, it is also entered in the book of God's remembrance "that we are believers:" and this appearing, we are graciously discharged, yea, rewarded, as if we ourselves had been perfectly innocent and obedient."

In concluding the present chapter, we wish again to call the attention of the reader to the intimate connection which exists between the doctrine of justification and most of the other doctrines which have been brought to view in the preceding pages. Though this has been already alluded to, when speaking of imputation and original sin, the truth of the remark was not, perhaps, so obvious as it must be now. The federal headship of Adam, the imputation of the guilt of his first sin to his posterity, original sin, the atonement and justification, are so closely connected, that if we have incorrect views with regard to the one, we shall err respecting the others. The views concerning these doctrines which we regard as scriptural, and which we have endeavoured to substantiate, so far as the design of the work would permit, are all different parts of the same system. If one of them be materially modified or denied, it involves a similar modification or denial of the whole. "While men are disputing," says Dr. Bellamy, "against the original constitution with Adam,* they unawares undermine the second constitution, which is the foundation of all

---

* Dr. Bellamy's views concerning God's covenant with Adam, original sin, &c., are the same with those of President Edwards; from whom extracts on this subject have been given.—See *True Religion Delineated*, pp. 269, 271.

our hopes. Eager to avoid Adam's first sin, whereby comes condemnation, they render of none effect Christ's righteousness, whereby comes justification." . . . . "What remains, therefore, but deism and infidelity?"

Truth is harmonious. The several doctrines of the Bible, like the stones in Solomon's temple, unite together, without the use of an "axe or hammer," to pare down their edges. But if one be rejected, there is not only a vacancy left in the building, which no art or ingenuity can supply, but the edifice itself is in danger of falling.

CHAPTER VII.

HUMAN ABILITY, REGENERATION, AND THE INFLUENCES OF THE HOLY SPIRIT.

THAT the fall of man has not released us from obligation to love and obey God, is maintained by all. This, however, it is believed, is perfectly consistent with the doctrine, that from our "original corruption, we are utterly indisposed, disabled, and made opposite to all good, and wholly inclined to all evil." As our inability is not only our misfortune, but our *sin*, it can never destroy moral obligation. Upon these points Calvinistic writers are generally agreed. But as the subject is attended with difficulties, which some have been anxious to avoid, a distinction has been resorted to between *natural* and *moral* inability; the latter of which, it is supposed, is the inability under which the sinner lies; and that he still possesses *natural* ability to do his duty. By this it is meant that he merely has the *physical powers*, or the *faculties of mind*, which are requisite to enable him to do what God requires—but that his mind is, nevertheless, *wholly disinclined* to that which is good; or, in other words, that he is *morally unable* to exercise holy affections. This distinction, it might be easily shown, is not without foundation; and yet when applied to the subject of religion, it is doubted by many, whether its use really solves any difficulties, or is productive of any practical good; chiefly from the ambiguity of the terms, and their liability to be misunderstood.

It is no part of our present purpose to discuss this question. We have introduced it in order to prepare the way for the observation, that those whose sentiments we are now considering, retain the term *natural* in connection with ability; and thus *appear* to accord with those who are in the habit of making the distinction to which we have referred; though in reality they occupy very different ground. Though when they speak of ability, they frequently annex to it the word *natural*, they seldom speak of *in*ability at all—but produce the impression that the ability which they preach is fully adequate to enable the sinner, independently of divine grace, to do all that God requires.

This was the opinion of Dr. Porter concerning Dr.

Beecher's preaching, prior to 1829. In a letter addressed to him which has been published in various papers, he says, "You exalt one part of Calvinism, viz: *human agency*, so as virtually to lose sight of its correlate *human dependence*, and thus make regeneration so much a result of *means* and instrumentality, that the sinner is born rather 'of blood or of the will of man than of God.'"

A similar opinion has been formed by some concerning his "Views in Theology," published in 1836. Dr. Harvey says concerning them, "Dr. Beecher's *Views*, it is true, have many shades and shadows of orthodoxy. The superstructure looks fair and imposing; but the philosophy is Pelagian, and all the orthodoxy in his '*Views*' is undermined by a false theory of moral agency, on which the whole is founded."—*Harvey on Moral Agency*, p. 6. The following quotations will show what foundation Dr. Harvey had for this opinion.

Dr. Beecher says, (p. 30, 31,) "That man possesses since the fall the powers of agency requisite to obligation, *on the ground of the possibility of obedience*, is a matter of notoriety. Not one of the powers of mind which constituted ability before the fall has been obliterated by that event. All that has ever been conceived, or that can now be conceived, as entering into the constitution of a free agent, capable of choosing life or death, or which did exist in Adam when he could and did obey, yet mutable, survived the fall." He says, (p. 31, 32,) "Choice, in its very nature, implies the possibility of a *different or*

contrary election to that which is made. There is always an *alternative* to that which the mind decides on with the conscious *power of choosing either."* ....
"The question of free will is not whether man *chooses*—this is notorious, none deny it; but whether his choice is free as opposed to a fatal necessity." Again, (p. 35,) "Choice, without the possibility of other or contrary choice, is the immemorial doctrine of fatalism:" and further, (p. 47,) "This doctrine of the *natural ability of choice, commensurate with obligation*, has been, and is, the received doctrine of the universal orthodox church, from the primitive age down to this day."

The first of these propositions speaks without any qualification of the *"possibility of obedience,"* in reference to fallen man—and makes this essential to obligation. The second and third predicate this possibility of obedience upon the possession of a *self-determining power of the will*, by which we can not only *choose*, but *alter our volitions* at pleasure. This, according to his view, is essential to free agency. The third affirms that "this *natural ability of choice*," by which we understand him to mean the power which we naturally possess as free agents, over our volitions, *"is commensurate with obligation."* If these are the ideas which he intends to convey, it follows, that man since the fall possesses all the powers which are requisite to enable him to change his sinful volitions for those which are holy: or, to use the language of Dr. Harvey, "that man possesses, since the fall, the powers of agency requisite to obligation, on the ground of possessing a power of contrary choice, by which he can recover himself from perfect sinfulness to perfect holiness."—*Harvey on Moral Agency*, pp. 80, 81. "Natural ability of choice, commensurate with obligation," says Dr. Harvey, "must mean something more than the mere power of choice; it means natural ability not only to do right, if one is disposed, but natural ability to overcome every moral impediment. In other words, it means natural ability to overcome moral inability, or natural ability which can produce ability enough to overcome moral inability. Thus, as I have before had occasion to remark, the great object is to render man, in his fallen state, independent of the grace of God. To accomplish this purpose, Dr. Beecher introduces the extra power of contrary choice as an addition to the simple power of choice, and which he deems sufficient to equal obligation, and if so, to bring the sinner out of darkness into light, to raise him from death to life. Thus Dr. Beecher, in effect, coincides with Pelagius, who denied all moral inability. Pelagius takes the city by undermining and sinking the wall; Dr. Beecher by building an embankment which shall overtop the wall. One sinks the wall to the surface, the other raises the surface to the wall's top; and in both cases, the obstacle of moral inability is annihilated."—*Harvey on Moral Agency*, pp. 115, 116.

We have exhibited Dr. Beecher's views in the above form, because the language of his several propositions is such, that the sentiments intended to be conveyed are not perfectly obvious upon a simple perusal. The deductions which we have made, or which we have quoted from Dr. Harvey, we do not of course, ascribe to Dr. Beecher, as expressing what he believes—but if we have not mistaken his views, they appear to lead, by legitimate consequence, to these conclusions—and to *some* of them it is probable he would not refuse his assent; since it would be going no further than has been expressed by two or three who belong to the same school.

Says Mr. Duffield—"Not much less deluding are the system and tactics of those who, fearing to invade the province of the Spirit, are careful to remind the sinner, that he is utterly unable by his own unassisted powers either to believe or to repent to the saving of his soul. It might as truly be said, that he cannot rise and walk, by his own unassisted powers."—*Duffield on Regeneration*, p. 542.

Mr. Finney's language is that "as God requires men to make themselves a new heart, on pain of eternal death, it is the strongest possible evidence that they are *able* to do it—to say he has commanded them to do it, without telling them they are *able*, is consummate trifling." . . . . . "If the sinner ever has a new heart, he must obey the command of the text, and make it himself." . . . . . . "Sinner! instead of waiting and praying for God to change your heart, you should at once summon up your powers, put forth the effort, and change the governing preferences of your mind. But here, some one may ask, Can the carnal mind, which is enmity against God, change itself? I have already said that this text in the original, reads, 'The minding of the flesh is enmity against God.' This minding of the flesh then, is a choice or preference to gratify the flesh. Now it is indeed absurd to say, that a choice can change itself; but it is not absurd to say, that the agent who exercises this choice can change it. The sinner that minds the flesh, can change his mind, and mind God."—*Sermons on Important Subjects*, pp. 18, 37, 38.

This exposition of the "carnal mind" is a favourite one with writers of this class. Says Mr. Barnes, "The amount of his [Paul's] affirmation is simply, that the *minding of the flesh*, the supreme attention to its dictates and desires, is not and cannot be subject to the law of God. They are wholly contradictory and irreconcilable." . . . . "But whether the *man himself* might not obey the law, whether *he* has, or has not, ability to do it, is a question which the Apostle does not touch, and on which this passage should not be adduced."—*Notes on the Romans*, p. 164. In commenting on the phrase, "neither indeed can be," he repeats the same sentiment concerning ability which is expressed above. Also in his exposition of the passage, "when we were without strength Christ died for the ungodly." "The remark of the Apostle here," says he, "has reference *only* to the condition of the race *before* an atonement was made. It does not pertain to the question whether man has strength to repent and to believe, after an atonement *is* made, which is a very different inquiry." Though Mr. Barnes expresses himself with much more caution than Messrs. Finney and Duffield, it is apparent that he favours their sentiments.

There is so striking a similarity between the views of these men and those of Dr. John Taylor of Norwich, England, a Socinian, that it will be appropriate to refer to the latter, with the remarks of President Edwards upon them, showing what he thought of their tendency. They are contained in his work on Original Sin. "It will follow," says he, "on our author's principles [Dr. Taylor's principles] not only with respect to infants, but even *adult* persons, that that redemption is *needless,* and Christ is dead in vain. Not only is there no need of Christ's redemption in order to deliverance from any consequences of *Adam's* sin, but also in order to perfect freedom from *personal* sin, and all its evil consequences. For God has made other sufficient provision for that, viz. *a sufficient power and ability, in all mankind, to do all their duty and wholly to avoid sin.* Yea, he insists upon it, that 'when men have not sufficient power to do their duty, they have *no* duty to do. We may safely and assuredly conclude, (says he,) that mankind in all parts of the world, have SUFFICIENT power to do the duty which God requires of them; and that he requires of them NO MORE than they have SUFFICIENT powers to do.' And in another place, 'God has given powers EQUAL to the duty which he expects.' And he expresses a great dislike at R. R's supposing 'that our propensities to evil and temptations are too strong to be EFFECTUALLY and CONSTANTLY resisted; or that we are unavoidably sinful IN A DEGREE; that our appetites and passions will be breaking out, notwithstanding our everlasting watchfulness.' These things fully imply that men have in their own natural ability sufficient means to avoid sin, and to be perfectly free from it; and so from all the bad consequences of it. And if the means are *sufficient*, then there is no need of more; and therefore there is no need of Christ's dying in order to it. What Dr. Taylor says, fully implies that it would be unjust in God to give mankind being in such circumstances, as that they would be more likely to sin, so as to be exposed to final misery, than otherwise. Hence then, without Christ and his redemption, and without any grace at all, MERE JUSTICE makes *sufficient provision* for our being free from sin and misery by our own power."

"If all mankind, in all parts of the world, have sufficient power to do their whole duty, without being sinful *in any degree*, then they have sufficient power to obtain righteousness by the law: and then, according to the apostle Paul, *Christ is dead in vain.* Gal. ii. 21. 'If righteousness come by law, Christ is dead in vain;'—*by law*, or the rule of right action, as our author explains the phrase. And according to the sense in which he explains this very place, 'it would have frustrated, or rendered useless, the grace of God, if Christ died to accomplish what was or MIGHT have been effected by law itself without his death. 'So that it most clearly follows from his own doctrine, *that Christ is dead in vain*, and the grace of God is *useless.* The same apostle says, *If there had been a law which* COULD *have given life, verily righteousness should have been by the law,* Gal. iii. 21; i. e. (according to Dr. Taylor's own sense,) if there was a law, that man, in his present state, had sufficient power to fulfil. For Dr. Taylor supposes the reason why the law could not give life, to be 'not because it was weak in itself, but through the weakness of our flesh, and the infirmity of human nature in the present state.' But he says, 'We are under a mild dispensation of GRACE making allowance for our infirmities.' By *our infirmities,* we may, on good ground, suppose he means that infirmity of human nature, which he gives as the reason why the law cannot give life. But what *grace* is there for making that allowance for our infirmities, which *justice* itself (according to his doctrine,) most absolutely requires, as he supposes divine justice exactly proportions our duty to our ability?

"Again, if it be said, that although Christ's redemption was not necessary to preserve men from *beginning to sin,* and getting into a course of sin, because they have sufficient power in themselves to avoid it; yet it may be necessary to deliver men, *after* they have by their own folly brought themselves under the *dominion* of evil appetites and passions; I answer, if it be so, that men need deliverance from those habits and passions which are become too strong for them, yet that deliverance, on our author's principles, would be no salvation from *sin.* For the exercise of passions which are too strong for us, and which we cannot overcome, is *necessary:* and he strongly urges, that a necessary evil can be no *moral* evil. It is true it is the *effect* of evil, as it is the effect of a bad practice, while the man had power to have avoided it. But then, according to Dr. Taylor, that evil *cause* alone is sin; for he expressly says, '*The cause of* every effect is alone chargeable with the effect it produceth, or which proceedeth from it.' And as to that sin which was the *cause*, the man needed no Saviour from *that*, having had *sufficient power* in himself to have avoided it. So that it follows by our author's scheme, that *none* of mankind, neither infants nor adult persons, neither the more or or less vicious, neither *Jews* nor *Gentiles*, neither *heathens* nor *Christians*, ever did or even could stand in any *need* of a Saviour; and that with respect to *all*, the truth is, *Christ is dead in vain.*

"If any should say, although all mankind in all ages have sufficient ability to do their whole duty, and so may by their own power enjoy perfect freedom from sin, yet God *foresaw* that they *would sin*, and that *after* they had sinned they would need Christ's death; I answer, it is plain, by what the apostle says in those places which were just now mentioned, (Gal. ii. 21, and iii. 21,) that God would have esteemed it needless to give his Son to die for men, unless there had been a prior impossibility of their having righteousness by any law; and that *if there had been a law which* COULD *have given life,* this other way by the death of Christ would not have been provided. And this appears agreeable to our author's own sense of things, by his words which have been cited, wherein he says, 'It would have FRUSTRATED or rendered USEless the grace of God, if Christ died to accomplish what was or MIGHT HAVE BEEN effected by law itself, without his death.'"

The new views concerning human ability have an exact counterpart in the description which is given by different writers of this school, of the work of regeneration, and the agency of the Holy Spirit. According to them, regeneration consists in the mere change of the governing purpose or preference of the soul—by which the sinner renounces the world as the supreme object of pursuit, and makes choice of God and heavenly things. Prompted by self-love, or in other words, by a constitutional desire for happiness, which is neither sinful nor holy, and the selfish principle in his heart being suspended, he enters upon a serious consideration and comparison of the various objects of happiness, until he discovers the infinite superiority of God and divine things to every other object. Then, by "desperate efforts," he fixes his heart upon them, and thus becomes a Christian. The part which the Holy Spirit performs in the work is, to present truth powerfully before the mind in the form of motives, like an advocate arguing a cause before a jury; or as one man influences and persuades another in the common affairs of life; though with infinitely greater skill and force than can be employed by any human agent. His attention is thus arrested—he revolves in his mind the points at issue—and at length being convinced where his true interest lies, he is prevailed upon by the moral suasion of the Spirit, to change the governing purpose or preference of his mind, and to choose God as his supreme portion.

The language of Dr. Taylor is as follows: "We proceed to say then, that before the act of the will or heart in which the sinner first prefers God to any other object, the object of the preference must be viewed or estimated as the greatest good. Before the object can be viewed as the greatest good, it must be compared with other objects, as both are sources or means of good. Before this act of comparing, there must be an act dictated not by selfishness but *self-love*, in which the mind determines to direct its thoughts to the objects for the sake of considering their relative value, of forming a judgment respecting it; and of choosing one or the other as the chief good."—*Christian Spectator*, 1829, pp. 19, 20.

"Divine truth does not become a means to this end, until the selfish principle so long cherished in the heart is suspended; and the mind is left to the control of that constitutional desire of happiness which is an original principle of our nature. Then it is, we apprehend, that God and the world are contemplated by the mind as objects of choice, substantially as they would be by a being who had just entered on existence, and who was called upon for the first time to select the one or the other as his supreme good." —*Christian Spectator*, 1829, p. 210.

"Now we readily concede that sinners never use the means of regeneration with a holy heart, nor with an unholy or sinful heart. But does it therefore follow that they never use them with any heart *at all?* What is that heart with which God in his law requires sinners to love him? Surely not a heart which is holy before they love him. Still less with a sinful heart; and yet he requires them to love him with some heart, even *their* heart. Is this no heart at all? We think on the contrary it is a *real* heart, a heart with which sinners can love God, even *without the grace of the Spirit*, and certainly with it."—*Christian Spectator*, 1830, pp. 149, 150.

Concerning the nature of the Spirit's agency, we believe Dr. Taylor has not published his views. But the author of "Letters on the New-Haven Theology" informs us that his sentiments correspond with those of Mr. Finney.

Mr. Finney says, "The Spirit pours the expostulation home with such power, that the sinner turns. Now, in speaking of this change, it is perfectly proper to say, that the Spirit turned him, just as you would say of a man who had persuaded another to change his mind on the subject of politics, that he had converted him and brought him over." . . . . . . "He does not act by direct physical contact upon the mind, but he uses the truth as his sword to pierce the sinner; and the motives presented in the gospel are the instruments he uses to change the sinner's heart. Some have doubted this, and supposed that it is equivalent to denying the Spirit's agency altogether to maintain that he converts sinners by motives. Others have denied the possibility of changing the heart by motives. But did not the serpent change Adam's heart by motives? and cannot the Spirit of God with infinitely higher motives exert as great power over mind as he can?" .... "From these remarks it is easy to answer the question sometimes put by individuals who seem to be entirely in the dark on this subject, whether in converting the soul the Spirit acts directly on the mind, or on the truth. This is the same nonsense as if you should ask whether an earthly advocate who had gained his cause, did it by acting directly and physically on the jury or on his argument." ..... "The power which God exerts in the conversion of a soul is *moral* power; it is that kind of power by which a statesman sways the mind of a senate; or by which an advocate moves and bows the heart of a jury."—*Sermons on Important Subjects*, pp. 21, 27, 28, 30.

As to what regeneration consists in, Mr. Finney observes: "A change of heart, then, consists in changing the controlling preference of the mind in regard to the *end* of pursuit. The selfish heart is a preference of self-interest to the glory of God and the interests of his kingdom. A new heart consists in a preference of the glory of God and the interests of his kingdom to one's own happiness." ... "It is a change in the choice of a *Supreme Ruler*."—*Ibid.* pp. 9, 10. In describing the process by which the sinner effects this change, he occupies nearly a whole sermon, which we cannot of course, with propriety, transfer to these pages. It corresponds substantially with the views already given from Dr. Taylor.

Mr. Duffield's account of regeneration is as follows: "It is going altogether beyond the analogy in the case, to assert that there is in regeneration the *injection, infusion,* or *implantation,* or *creation* of a *new principle of spiritual life.*" . . . . "Whenever the Spirit of God excites and secures in the mind and heart of man those acts and emotions which are appropriate to his rational soul, i. e. when they are directed to God, as his supreme good and chief end, he is renewed, regenerated, born again."—*Work on Regeneration,* pp. 202, 203, 204. But how does the Spirit produce this result?" According to him it is done by moral suasion. He has two whole chapters, occupying thirty-five pages, entitled "The Moral Suasion of the Spirit." In one of these he illustrates his views of the nature of the Spirit's agency by the power of persuasion exerted by one man over another, and the greater success which a man of "practical knowledge and tact and particular acquaintance with dispositions," &c. has above one who is less skilful. "Shall we suppose, (says he,) that God cannot do with sinners in reference to himself what one man has done with another?—that a physical efficiency is necessary to make the sinner willing to confide in him and repent of his rebellion? To suppose this, is in fact to attribute a moral influence to a man more potent than that which, in such a case, it would be requisite God should exert! It would in effect be to say that *man* can subdue *his* foe, and by an appropriate moral influence convert him into a friend; but that God *cannot* convert *his* enemy, and bring him to believe, *except* he puts forth his physical power and literally creates him over again." Pp. 492, 493.*

During the progress of the discussion concerning the New Theology, it was alleged by some, by way of objection to the new theory, that it involved the principle that regeneration is not an *instantaneous* but a *gradual* work. This allegation, so far as I recollect, was for a time neither admitted nor denied. But recently the doctrine of *gradual* regeneration has been avowed. Mr. Gilbert,† of Wilmington, Delaware, published in the *Philadelphian* in 1833, a number of communications on this subject; which were afterwards revised and enlarged, and in 1836, at the "earnest request" of the "members of the Ministers' Meeting of New Castle County, Delaware," were published in a pamphlet form, under the title of "Moral Suasion; or Regeneration not a Mira-

* This power of moral suasion is the kind of influence referred to by a certain preacher who said, "If I were as eloquent as the Holy Ghost I could convert sinners as well as He." In the *National Preacher* for February 1832, a sermon furnished by Dr. Griffin commences by quoting the above remark. It being attributed by some to a Presbyterian minister of my acquaintance, I asked him whether he had ever used this expression. He replied that he had, and vindicated its correctness; though he said it did not appear in the connection in which he used it, as it does when standing by itself.

† In the organization of the New-school General Assembly in May, 1838, Mr. Gilbert was chosen permanent clerk.

cle," &c. It is dedicated to the members of the Ministers' Meeting, and to the elders of the churches under their pastoral charge. These facts appear to show that Mr. Gilbert's views accord with the sentiments of the other ministers with whom he is associated in that State, and that they *desire* to have them prevail throughout their churches.

Mr. Gilbert affirms that " the Bible knows no *instantaneous regeneration;* this is a refinement of theological philosophers. Being born again, and changing the heart of stone to a heart of flesh, is a *gradual process;* although under some circumstances it may be a very *short one.*" The remark of Dr. Griffin, that "motives can never change an *unholy temper,*" &c. he calls "strange philosophy; flying not only in the face of Scripture, but of every day matters of fact." "How often," (says he,) "do we see *enmity* to a neighbour, corrected, moderated, subdued and turned to love, by proper motives presented to the mind? And enmity to God is restrained and subdued in the same manner." These motives, he maintains, are presented in the latter case by the Holy Spirit, who convicts, converts, and sanctifies, "by the influence of truth presented to the mind and in no other way." In one place, he says: "*Regeneration cannot be wrought without the truth. It is in view of the truth, through the truth, and by the truth, the soul is convicted, converted, and sanctified from beginning to end.*"

To illustrate his views he has furnished a diagram consisting of an arc of a circle, in the centre of which he has placed the Holy Spirit. From this centre are drawn straight lines to various points in the arc, representing truth as employed by the Spirit. A sinner pursuing his way to hell is represented as being met by one of these lines, through the influence of which he is persuaded to diverge a little from the path he was pursuing, and proceeding at an angle of about forty-five degrees, he passes gradually through the several steps of conviction, regeneration, and sanctification, describing in his progress the arc of the circle; until arriving at a point directly opposite from where he started, he becomes perfect and ascends to heaven.

That the reader may see for himself this new and improved method of regeneration by attraction, we will give the diagram with the author's explanation.* We ought to remark, however, that he uses the terms *conviction* and *sanctification* in accommodation to the views and language of others. According to his own views the whole process from beginning to end belongs to the work of regeneration. "By *regeneration*," says he, "is understood the divine agency in the *whole process* of a sinner's conviction and conversion; but in this discussion I use it as it is used by Dr. Griffin, Mr. Smith and others, in the *restricted sense* as distinguished from previous conviction and subsequent sanctification." "It [the Bible] knows of no regeneration as distinct from conviction and the beginning of sanctification."

---

* As a matter of taste we would exclude this diagram from our pages—but other considerations which we regard as paramount, induce us to insert it.

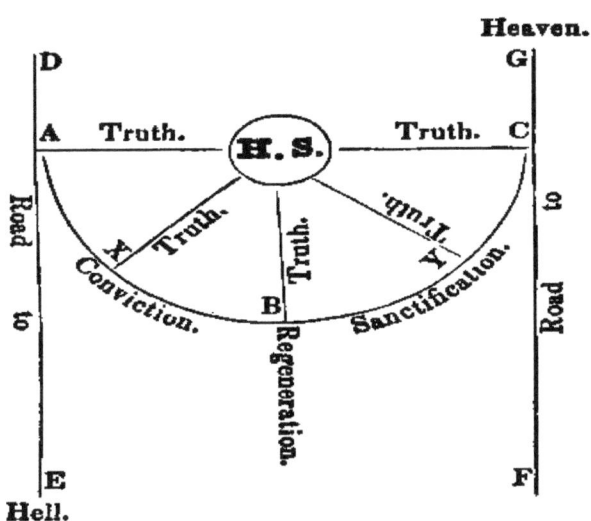

THE AUTHOR'S EXPLANATION.

"Let the semicircle, A B C, represent the sinner's course from sin to holiness. Let D E represent the road to hell, in which the impenitent sinner is found by the Holy Spirit, and influenced at the point A by a new presentation of truth, to stop and turn gradually from his downward course, through the curve of conviction, towards the point B when his conviction becoming perfect and irresistible, he *yields* and *turns* from his downward course, through the process of sanctification, until at C (or at death,) becoming perfect, he flies off, if you please, in a tangent, to heaven. Till he reaches the point B though turning gradually from the more direct road to hell, he is still in the downward course, and should the

Spirit let go of him, at any point, he flies off, by his own centrifugal force, in a moment towards perdition. *The point B represents what these writers call 'Regeneration.'*"

"The Holy Spirit, like the sun in the centre, is the source of all right motion; and the power by which he attracts or influences the sinner, is the power of truth, or moral motive; by which the moral agent is checked at A, and moved and controlled through the whole course from A to C. It is understood, of course, that the whole process may be longer or shorter, according to circumstances; may begin and be perfected, as with the thief on the cross, in a single day; or as in the case of Methuselah, may occupy nine hundred or one thousand years. Conviction, also, may be short, and sanctification long, or the reverse. But conviction must, from the nature of the case, precede regeneration, or regeneration cannot be a rational change. A physical change may take place without conviction; but physical regeneration is a thing which I cannot comprehend, any more than physical conviction or physical sanctification. The doctrine of the moral suasionists is, that the *influence which convicts, also regenerates and sanctifies.* That the same power which moves the sinner from A to B moves him through the point B and along the line to C. And that the whole change is wrought through appropriate means, without a miracle, by the Holy Spirit."

Agreeably to these ideas of gradual progress from the first point to the last, he says: "There is very little distinction between the last degree of sin and the lowest degree of holiness; between the last exercise of an unconverted and the first of a converted man; between the last feeble struggle of selfishness and the first feeble exercise of love." . . . . "There is a great difference between supreme selfishness and supreme love *in their extremes;* but between the last feeble influence of selfishness and the first feeble exercise of love to God, the difference is as imperceptible, as between the *adjacent sides of the equatorial line.*" . . . . "The point B on the diagram represents the transition line. And it may be asked, Is it not an important one? I answer, Yes. Important on many accounts, but not because of any *special influence* used then, but like the equator, as a measure of relative progress, and as the *era of a great change in all our moral relations and circumstances.* Like the equatorial line, however, it is *in itself* of no consequence at all."

If this were not a subject too serious for ridicule, Mr. Gilbert might be successfully assailed by this weapon. He has fairly exposed himself to this mode of attack. But if I possessed a talent for the humorous, and were disposed to indulge in it, I feel too much shocked at his method of illustration to treat it with ridicule. He appears to have felt himself, that he would run "the risk of being counted very presumptuous;" and I doubt not he was correct in his apprehensions. A majority of his readers, it seems to me, (unless they belong to a particular class) will feel that he has "trodden on holy ground," without "taking his shoes from off his feet;" that he has "put forth his hand and touched the ark of God," without "sanctifying himself;" or in other words, that he has so presented the subject, as to make him appear almost profane.

This very circumstance, however, serves to show the fallacy of these new doctrines. Mr. Gilbert uses no irreverent language—he does not caricature the New Theology. The views expressed by different writers as quoted in the present chapter, if carried out to their full extent, and illustrated by a diagram, could not perhaps be exhibited more accurately than by that which has been presented. But a description given in words, which have often an equivocal or doubtful import, produces not only a less vivid, but a less accurate impression than that which is made by a figure faithfully drawn and presented to the eye. This remark is true not only in reference to landscapes, &c., but to a certain extent in regard to moral and religious truth. Mr. Gilbert has shown by his diagram, that it is capable of being employed in the present instance; and possibly it may be of service to the cause of truth, by showing in a more striking manner than can be exhibited by quoting their language, the dangerous extremes to which those men are tending. Give not only words but *visibility* to their doctrines—let them be *seen* as well as heard—and they will arouse the feelings of many who have not before been seriously alarmed.

CHAPTER VIII.

HUMAN ABILITY, REGENERATION, &C., CONTINUED FROM THE PRECEDING CHAPTER.

WE observed in chapter fifth that the New Theology concerning the nature of sin and holiness, viz: that they consist in acts, involves a new theory of regeneration. What this theory is may be learned from the statements made in the preceding chapter. It is the following: That in regeneration no *principle* of holiness is implanted in the soul, prior to the exercise of holy acts, from which principle, or "moral state of the soul," those acts proceed; but that the whole change consists in the *acts* of the soul itself; which from having been sinful now become holy. A previous holy relish or taste, which, according to the old doctrine, is essential in order to give to these acts a holy character, is regarded by these new system-makers, as unphilosophical and absurd; involving what they term physical regeneration, passivity, &c.

If by physical regeneration is meant a mechanical change in the substance of the soul, it forms no part of the Old Theology. But if it mean a direct agency of the Spirit upon the soul, by which its faculties are so renewed, that it receives the principles of a new and holy life, and therefore may be properly said to possess a new nature, it is what I understand to be the true doctrine. "The scriptural representations of conversion, (says President Edwards,) strongly imply and signify a change of nature; such as *being born again; becoming new creatures; rising from the dead; being renewed in the spirit of the mind; dying to sin, and living to righteousness; putting off the old man and putting on the new man; being ingrafted into a new stock; having a divine seed implanted in the heart; being made partakers of the divine nature,"* &c. . . . . "He [God] gives his Spirit to be united to the faculties of the soul and to *dwell there* as a principle of spiritual life and activity. He not only actuates the soul, but he abides in it. The mind thus endued with grace is possessed of a new nature."—*Edwards on the Affections.*

That the soul is passive in regeneration, is the doctrine of our standards—and it necessarily results from the preceding view concerning the nature of the change. In the chapter on Effectual Calling, both are presented in connection with each other. The change itself is declared to consist in "enlightening the minds [the minds of those whom he effectually calls] spiritually and savingly, to understand the things of God, taking away their heart of stone, and giving unto them a heart of flesh; renewing their wills, &c. It is then added, in the next section, "This effectual call is of God's free and special grace alone, not from anything at all foreseen in man, who is altogether passive therein, until being quickened and renewed by the Holy Spirit," &c. The former part of this quotation exhibits the implantation of a holy principle, or the change of our natures, by conferring spiritual illumination, removing the heart of stone and giving a heart of flesh, and by renewing the will. The latter affirms that this new nature was not imparted to us by our own agency, but by God, who works upon us by his Holy Spirit, to quicken and renew us; and that we must of course, as to this particular point in the history of the change, be the passive recipients of divine grace—not bringing it about by our own acts, but being acted upon by the renovating power of God.

This doctrine, however, does not imply that we are not to be active beforehand in the diligent use of the means of grace—nor that we are inactive at the time, with respect to the effects of the change. Simultaneously with this change, and as the immediate consequence of it, the sinner is "persuaded and enabled to embrace Jesus Christ, as he is freely offered to him in the gospel." In this he is not passive, but active. When God "by his almighty power determines the sinner to that which is good," or in other words, gives him an apprehension of the excellence of divine things, and of the all-sufficiency of Christ as his Saviour, and thus "effectually draws" him to Christ, he comes, not reluctantly, but "most freely, being made willing by his grace." Regeneration, or the implanting of a holy principle, is the cause; and our conversion, or turning to God, is the effect. In the former we are passive, in the latter active. Though in the order of time they are simultaneous, in the order of nature the former is the antecedent, the latter the consequent; just as breathing, though simultaneous with the existence of life, is nevertheless the effect of it, and would never occur, unless life had been previously communicated.

Dr. Cox, who does not appear to have adopted all the principles of the New Theology, has expressed himself on the subject of regeneration in a manner very different from what has been customary among Calvinistic writers.* To the doctrine that "God creates or inserts some *holy principle* in us, which constitutes regeneration, and in which we are entirely passive, but that thereafter we actively do our duty," he strongly objects, and says "it can command the confidence of no well disciplined mind." He adds, it is true, "till we have both a definition of what is meant by *holy principle*, and a demonstration of its existence," &c.; and he wishes to have it understood that he does not object to its use, if explained in a particular way—but the doctrine, as it has been commonly received, he does not embrace. In his letter to the conductors of the Biblical Repertory, in reply to their review of his sermon, he asks, "Is not a Christian active in all his moral relations? In believing and obeying God? Certainly active in the total progress of religion, in the soul and life: then why not also in its rise? If active progressively,

---

* Since the publication of the first edition, Dr. Cox has published a series of numbers in the New York Evangelist, entitled "The Hexagon," in which he has discussed at length several important points of difference between the Old and New Schools, and sided strongly with the latter, maintaining their particular views of doctrine.

then why not initially too? If active in the work of sanctification, why not in the whole of it, in its commencement as well as its continuance; in regeneration as well as sanctification? *How is a man regenerated, but as he believes and obeys the gospel?* Is he regenerated *before* he does this? Is he more dependent in regeneration one whit than in sanctification?" What he terms the passivity doctrine, or the doctrine of passive regeneration, he explicitly and freely disavows.

The remarks of the editors of the Repertory, in their review of his sermon, are so much in point, that we shall transcribe a paragraph of considerable length, in the place of any further observations of ours upon this subject.

"As to the point which Dr. Cox thinks so 'intrinsically absurd,' and about which he says so much, whether a man is passive in regeneration, it will be seen that, for its own sake, it does not merit a moment's discussion. It depends entirely on the previous question. If regeneration be that act of the soul by which it chooses God for its portion, there is an end of all debate on the subject. For no one will maintain that the soul is passive in acting. But if there be any change in the moral state of the soul, prior to its turning unto God, then it is proper to say, that the soul is passive as to that particular point; that is, that the Holy Spirit is the author, and the soul the subject of the change. For all that is meant by the soul's being passive, is, that it is not the agent of the change in question. Its immediate and delightful turning unto God is its own act; the state of mind which leads to this act is produced directly by the Spirit of God. The whole question is, whether any such anterior change is necessary; whether a soul polluted and degraded by sin, or in Scripture language, carnal, needs any change in its moral taste before it can behold the loveliness of the divine character. For that this view must precede the exercise of affection, we presume will not be denied. If this point be decided, the propriety of using the word passive to denote that the soul is the subject and not the agent of the change in question, need not give us much trouble. Sure it is that this change is in Scripture always referred to the Holy Spirit. It is the soul that repents, believes, hopes and fears; but it is the Holy Spirit that regenerates. He is the author of our faith and repentance by inducing us to act, but no man regenerates himself. The soul, although essentially active, is still capable of being acted upon. It receives impressions from sensible objects, from other spirits, and from the Holy Ghost. In every sensation, there is an impression made by some external object, and the immediate knowledge which the mind takes of the impression. As to the first point, it is passive, or the subject; as to the second, it is active, or the agent. These two are indeed inseparably connected, and so are regeneration and conversion. . . . . And if the Holy Spirit does make such an impression on the mind, or exert such an influence as induces it immediately to turn to God, then it is correct to say that it is passive in regeneration, though active in conversion. However, this is a very subordinate point; the main question is, whether there is not a holy 'relish,' taste, or principle produced in the soul prior, in the order of nature, to any holy act of the soul itself. If Dr. Cox can show this to be 'intrinsically absurd,' we shall give up the question of 'passivity' without a moment's demur. To relinquish the other point, however, will cost us a painful struggle. It will be giving up the main point in debate between the friends and opposers of the doctrine of grace from Augustine to the present day. It will be the renunciation of what Calvinists, old and new, have believed to be the scriptural doctrine of original righteousness, original sin, and efficacious grace. It will be the rejection of that whole system of mingled sovereignty and love which has been the foundation, for ages, of so many hopes, and of so much blessedness to the people of God."

We mentioned in the last chapter that the New Theology involves the doctrine of *gradual* regeneration; and we quoted from Mr. Gilbert's pamphlet to show that this sentiment is now avowed by some of the advocates of the new system. On this point Dr. Griffin remarks, "The *evidence* of the change may be earlier or later in its appearance, and more or less rapid in its developments, but the change itself is always instantaneous. Is not such an idea more than implied in the text? [Ezek. xi. 19.] What is the blessing promised? Not the *gradual* improvement of an *old* temper, but "a *new* spirit;"—"the stony heart" not softened *by degrees* into flesh, but by one decisive effort removed, and a heart of flesh substituted in its room." . . . . "This doctrine, however, does not militate against the idea of an *antecedent preparation* in the conscience, wrought by the means of grace and the enlightening influences of the Spirit."—*Park Street Lectures*, pp. 91, 101.

These means according to our standards are "the word, sacraments, and prayer." In answer to the question, How is the word made effectual to salvation? the following answer is given: "The Spirit of God maketh the reading, but especially the preaching of the word, an effectual means of enlightening, convincing and humbling sinners, of driving them out of themselves, and drawing them unto Christ," &c. Thus the law is said to be "our schoolmaster to lead us to Christ;" "The law of the Lord is perfect, converting the soul;" "Of his own will begat he us, by the word of truth." But the word, let it be remembered, is only the *means*, which the Holy Spirit can employ or not as he pleases; and which when he does employ (as is usually the case) does not become effectual to salvation, till he by a direct influence upon the heart, prepares it to receive and embrace the truth. Lydia did not attend to the things spoken by Paul, until *"the Lord opened her heart."* In order that David might behold wondrous things out of God's law, he prayed that God would *"open his eyes."* The primitive Christians had access by faith into God's grace, and rejoiced in the hope of the glory of God, exercising the grace of patience in their tribulations, "because *the love of God was shed abroad in their hearts* by the Holy Ghost given unto them."

Though all these texts do not refer to regeneration in the *restricted* sense, they prove the doctrine of the *direct* influence of the Spirit upon the heart—and it is for this purpose we have referred to them. If the Spirit exerts an immediate influence upon the hearts of believers, in order to make the word effectual to their sanctification, much more on the hearts of sinners to make it effectual to their conversion. In the mind of the believer there is something congenial with the spirit of the gospel; something, therefore, for divine truth to act upon in the form of motives: but, to use the language of Dr. Griffin, "motives can never change an *unholy temper;* there is no tendency in truth to change a depraved '*taste.*' The change must take place before light can act."

This doctrine of the direct agency of the Spirit, and the implantation of a principle of holiness in the heart, is inseparably connected with the sentiment that the change is instantaneous. Motives operate gradually upon the mind; but the communication to the soul of a new spiritual taste, is the work of a moment. We either possess this holy temper or we do not; there is no point of time when we have neither enmity nor love; or when our affections are suspended in equilibrio between the two. Our souls are necessarily either in one state or its opposite; and our transition, therefore, from one to the other must be instantaneous; as when God said, "Let there be light, and there was light."

It may, perhaps, be thought by some that the difference between instantaneous and gradual regeneration is not important, since both recognize the necessity of becoming holy. But a little reflection will show the contrary. Gradual regeneration is founded on the principle that there is something good in the unregenerate man, which needs only to be fostered and cherished, in order to make him holy. Of course it involves a denial of total depravity, and of the necessity of an entire radical change of character. It fosters pride and self-righteousness; and produces hostility to those doctrines of grace which distinguish the gospel from the religion of nature. It is, in short, taking a step towards infidelity.

In regard to human ability, our Confession of Faith uses the following language: "Man, by his fall into a state of sin, hath wholly lost all ability of will to any spiritual good accompanying salvation; so as a natural man being altogether averse from that which is good, and dead in sin, is not able, by his own strength, to convert himself, or prepare himself thereunto." Some have endeavoured to prove from this passage that, according to the Confession of Faith, depravity belongs exclusively to the will. But this, it appears to me, is not a correct exposition. As the design of the chapter was to treat "Of Free Will," it would of course state explicitly what effect the fall had upon the will, without speaking, as a matter of course, concerning the other powers of the soul. There is, however, a clause introduced, which was evidently designed to refer to the whole moral man: *"Dead in sin."* The preceding clause, viz. "so as a natural man being altogether averse from that which is good," refers to the will; but to this, the other is superadded—"*and dead in sin*"—which was intended to convey an additional idea, embracing, perhaps, the former, but amplifying and extending it, so as to include the depravity of our whole nature. This will appear by a reference to the chapter on the "Fall of Man;" where it reads as follows: "By this sin they [our first parents] fell from their original righteousness, and communion with God, and so became dead in sin, and wholly defiled in all the faculties and parts of soul and body." It will also appear, by a reference to the chapter on "Effectual Calling;" where, in describing the manner in which we are brought "out of that state of sin and death," it is not only said that our wills are renewed, but our minds spiritually and savingly enlightened to understand the things of God; and our heart of stone taken away and a heart of flesh given unto us. If depravity belongs to the will only, that alone needs to be operated upon in effectual calling. It is evident, therefore, that our standards teach the doctrine not only that the will is depraved, but likewise "all the faculties of the soul."

This view also accords with Scripture. "There is none that *understandeth*." Rom. iii. 11. "Having the *understanding darkened*, being alienated from the life of God through the ignorance that is in them, because of the *blindness* of their heart." Eph. iv. 18. "But the natural man receiveth not the things of the Spirit of God, for they are foolishness unto him;

neither can he know them, because they are spiritually discerned." 1 Cor. ii. 14. Here it is manifest that our depravity affects the understanding. Hence in conversion it is necessary that we be enlightened to discern spiritual things. "The eyes of your understanding being enlightened." Eph. i. 18. "For God who commanded the light to shine out of darkness, hath shined in our hearts, to give the light of the knowledge of the glory of God in the face of Jesus Christ." 2 Cor. iv. 6. "And have put on the new man, which is renewed in knowledge after the image of him that created him." Col. iii. 10.

Depravity is also predicated of the heart and conscience. "The heart is deceitful above all things, and desperately wicked." Jer. xvii. 9. "But unto them that are defiled and unbelieving, is nothing pure; but even their mind and conscience is defiled." Tit. i. 15. Do these texts refer exclusively to the will? or do they not include also the other moral powers? As the heart is the seat of the affections, to say that the heart is wicked, is equivalent to declaring the affections to be depraved and alienated from God. Accordingly, to change the heart is to give us a holy temper—to renew our affections. "The Lord thy God will circumcise thine heart, and the heart of thy seed, to love the Lord thy God." Deut. xxx. 6. "And I will put a new spirit within you, and I will take the stony heart out of their flesh and will give them a heart of flesh." Ezek. xi. 19. When this is done, our conscience will likewise be rectified. "Having our hearts sprinkled from an evil conscience." Heb. x. 22.

Then, too, the will which is controlled by the state of the heart, is sweetly inclined by the same Spirit to choose and rest upon Christ as the portion of the soul. "My people shall be *willing* in the day of thy power." Psa. cx. 3.

From this view of the subject, it appears that the fall has affected the whole moral man. What God says of Judah is applicable to all mankind. "The whole head is sick, and the whole heart faint. From the sole of the foot even unto the head, there is no soundness in it." Isa. i. 5, 6. This doctrine, we admit, is very humiliating, and calculated to make the sinner feel his dependence upon God. But this, instead of being an objection, is a proof of its correctness. While it must not be so interpreted as to annihilate or even impair the sinner's obligation, or form any excuse for his impenitence and unbelief, it is a doctrine which is pre-eminently adapted to drive him from those refuges of self-righteousness and self-sufficiency, which prove the ruin of so many souls, and lead him to seek salvation only through the grace and righteousness of Jesus Christ. It is, indeed, the very point to which sinners always come before they embrace the Saviour.

On this subject Dr. Witherspoon uses the following language: "On a conviction of our own inability, one would think we should but the more humbly and the more earnestly apply to Him, who is all-sufficient in power and grace. The deplorable and naturally helpless state of sinners, doth not hinder exhortations to them in Scripture; and therefore takes not away their obligation to duty. See an address, where the strongest metaphors are retained, the exhortation given in these very terms, and the foundation of the duty plainly pointed out: 'Wherefore he saith, Awake thou that sleepest, and arise from the dead, and Christ shall give thee light.' From which it is very plain, that the moral inability, under which sinners now lie, as a consequence of the fall, is not of such a nature as to take 'away the guilt of sin, the propriety of exhortation to duty, or the necessity of endeavours after recovery." . . . . . . "I make no scruple to acknowledge, that it is impossible for me; nay, I find no difficulty in supposing that it is impossible for any finite mind, to point out the bounds between the 'dependence' and 'activity' of the creature." . . . . "The new birth is a 'supernatural change;' it is the effect of the power of God; it is the work of the Holy Ghost. I have been at the more pains to establish this truth, because I am persuaded, that until it be truly received there may be a form, but there can be nothing of the power of godliness." . . . . . . "But what shall we say? Alas! the very subject we are now speaking of affords a new proof of the blindness, prejudice, and obstinacy of sinners. They are self-condemned; for they do not act the same part in similar cases. The affairs of the present life are not managed in so preposterous a manner. He that ploughs his ground, and throws in his seed, cannot so much as unite one grain to the clod; nay, he is not able to conceive how it is done. He cannot carry on, nay, he cannot so much as begin one single step of this wonderful process towards the subsequent crop; the mortification of the seed, the resurrection of the blade, and gradual increase, till it come to perfect maturity. Is it, therefore, reasonable that he should say, 'I for my part can do nothing; it is, first and last, an effect of divine power and energy: and God can as easily raise a crop without sowing as with it; in a single instant, and in any place, as in a long time by the mutual influence of soil and season; I will therefore spare myself the hardship of toil and labour, and wait with patience till I see what he will be pleased to send?' Would not this be madness? Would it not be universally reputed so? And would it not be equal madness to turn the grace of God into licentiousness? Believe it, the warning is equally reasonable and equally necessary, in spiritual as in temporal things. 'Be not deceived, God is not mocked, for whatsoever a man soweth, that shall he also reap: for he that soweth to the flesh, shall of the flesh reap corruption; but he that soweth to the Spirit, shall of the Spirit reap life everlasting.' "—*Practical Treatise on Regeneration*, Sect. 4.

But while the doctrine of human inability and dependence upon God, as understood and believed by the friends of the Old Theology, does not destroy accountableness, nor impair obligation, nor discourage effort; but brings the sinner to his proper place, before the throne of divine mercy; we think the doctrine of *ability*, as maintained by the advocates of the New Theology, is calculated to produce such independence of feeling, with regard to the Spirit's influences, as to be a serious obstacle to genuine conversion. Among the "false comforts for sinners," which Mr. Finney enumerates, one is, "telling the sinner to *pray for a new heart.*" He asks, "Does God say, Pray for a new heart? Never. He says, 'Make you a new heart.' And the sinner is not to be told to pray to God to do his duty for him, but to go and do it himself."—*Lectures on Revivals*, p. 318. Thus it appears, we must not direct sinners to seek God for renewing grace, because they have sufficient ability of their own to perform the work. To preach to them the necessity of the Spirit's influences, while exhorting them to duty, would be according to him "unphilosophical." We must tell them "to go and do it themselves." What kind of conversions is such instruction as this calculated to produce?* It is no wonder that

---

* Let the reader judge of the probable effect upon the sinner of preaching such doctrines as are developed in the following conversation between a licentiate, a student from New Haven, and two highly respectable ministers, in 1832. It was taken down at the time by one of the ministers, as he has informed me, "the paper sealed up, and has been kept since a secret." In communicating it to me a few weeks ago, he observes: "If you judge it to be proper, you are now at liberty to use the document in your forthcoming book; suppressing the names for the present, but considering me as responsible for the statement, and ready to give the names hereafter if necessary."

"Mr. ———, [one of the ministers,] in the course of general conversation, alluded to New Haven as a school of Theology, and asked finally that Mr. ———, [the licentiate,] would state what were the peculiarities of *Professor Fitch's scheme of natural depravity.* Mr. ——— avowed himself a believer in that scheme, and stated among other things, in substance as fol-

the revivals of religion which have occurred within the last ten years, under the ministry of such men, should furnish so many examples of apostacy. In a lows: (many of the following views, he said, however, *were his own*, and not chargeable upon any others, or any particular school:) that 'moral character was predicated entirely on *choice between good and evil:* that man was not regarded with displeasure in the sight of God, either by *imputation of original sin*, or as having a disposition to evil. He was in no sense a sinner, until of sufficient age and capacity to choose for himself; and *if* there was a period in his existence previous to that, *during* that period he was an innocent being.'"

"The bearing of this on the doctrine of *regeneration* was then suggested; whereupon Mr. ———— stated in substance, that he did not regard the saying of Christ to Nicodemus, 'that which is born of the *flesh* is *flesh*, and that which is born of the *Spirit* is *spirit*,' as implying any thing like a new moral nature, opposite to his first nature, as given to him in regeneration. He believed that subject had been misunderstood. There was indeed a necessity for regeneration, but it consisted not in the implantation of new principles, but the rational turning of the same principles to a new course. *As to the way in which it was produced*, God's help was indeed necessary, but no more so than in every other action of man. He presented motives, and when a man sincerely made up his resolution to follow them, and did decide to do so, that was the beginning of a new life.' Mr. ———— asked him if any sinner ever did come to Christ without *feeling his helpless and lost condition?* Mr. ———— said 'he thought, *yes;* and mentioned his own case.'"

"The bearing of the subject on *atonement and justification* was next alluded to; and Mr. ———— [the licentiate,] observed 'that it was a scheme which did indeed run through the whole. As to atonement, he believed in it, but he semed to consider it as consisting in *what lay between God and his intelligent universe exclusively*, and that for *laying a ground of justifying his own proceedings;* as such, a man ought to trust in or believe

discourse delivered by Mr. Finney in Chatham street chapel, in 1836, are found such sentences as the fol-

the atonement: but in [the] matter of personal experience we had nothing to do with it; the righteousness of Christ is in no sense imputed to us: we must be accepted on the ground of our own obedience.'"

"Much was said also of *the practical influence* of such a style of preaching; and it was objected to Mr. ———'s scheme, that taking men as they are, they would be likely to interpret his views of their own powers and independency as even more favourable to themselves than he probably intended: and Mr. ——— [one of the ministers] remarked that as the gospel was represented 'to be a seeking and saving *that which was lost;*' 'to kill and make alive;' he had always felt it to be more necessary to show men their helplessness connected with their guilt, and a way of hope, than to persuade them of their own powers. Mr. ——— [the licentiate,] held the opposite opinion. He seemed to think that the reason why many more were not pious, was, *that too many and unnecessary difficulties were left in the way.* They ought to be *reasoned with more:* show them that this work is not *so hard and unreasonable:* they could be persuaded to make *a choice* if you would only present the thing as *rational;* and many were thus won, where this scheme was now adopted.' He said much of the figurative language of Scripture, and seemed to think that such passages as 'the carnal mind is enmity against God,' did not apply to men at the present age of the world, but peculiarly to the Jews, on account of their prejudices. The opposition which we have often witnessed against religion in natural men is not so much against God or religion itself, as against the prejudiced representations of it by mistaken teachers.'"

This individual, who is denominated by my correspondent "a *respectable* young man," was at that time, as I infer from his letter, seeking a settlement in a Presbyterian congregation.

lowing :* "You profess that you want to have sinners converted. But what avails it if they sink right back again into conformity to the world?" .... "Where are the proper results of the glorious revivals we have had?" ...... "The great body of them [the converts of the last ten years] are a disgrace to religion." .... "Of what use is it to convert sinners and make them such Christians as these?" This is an acknowledgment that the fruits of those revivals are not such as were anticipated—and so long as converts are made under the influence of such doctrines, and that system of measures which corresponds with them, we must expect similar results. Their goodness will be as the morning cloud, and as the early dew it will pass away.

The following remarks of Dr. Reed, one of the delegates from England to the American churches, accord with the sentiments and observation of very many in America, who have been "witnesses of these things." "The New Divinity and the New Measures have greatly coalesced, and they have given for the time, currency to each other. Many pious and ardent persons and preachers, from the causes to which I have adverted, were disposed to think that the new opinions had all the advantage in a revival, and this gave them all the preference in their judgment. Where they in connection with the New Measures have been

* We quote from the Literary and Theological Review. The sermon it appears was reported in the New York Evangelist, February 13, 1836.

vigorously applied, there has, indeed, been no want of excitement. The preacher who firmly believes that the conversion of men rests on the force of *moral suasion,* is not unlikely to be persuasive. And the hearer who is told 'he can convert himself,' that it is 'as easy for him to do so as to walk,' that he has only 'to resolve to do it and it is done,' is not unlikely to be moved into self-complacent exertion. But it may be asked, does either the preacher or the hearer possess those sentiments which are likely to lead to a true conversion, and to bring forth fruits meet for repentance?"

"By their fruits ye shall know them. There has certainly been good done where there has been much evil, for with this evil there has been a large portion of divine truth. But I fear not to say, that where there has been the largest infusion of the New Divinity into the New Measures, there has been the greatest amount of unwarrantable extravagance. There has been great excitement, much animal emotion and sympathy, high resolves, and multiplied conversions, *but time has tested them and they have failed.*"

CHAPTER IX.

A CONTRAST BETWEEN THE OLD AND NEW THEOLOGY, BY WAY OF REVIEW, AND A NOTICE OF THE PERFECTIONISM OF MR. FINNEY.

THAT the reader may see at a single view the most prominent points of difference between the Old and New Theology, we shall exhibit them in few words by way of contrast:—in doing which we shall take a kind of retrospect of the subject, and exemplify some of the principles which have been noticed, by a few additional quotations.

1. The Old Theology places God upon the throne of the universe, and makes him competent to say concerning all creatures and events, "My counsel shall stand, and I will do all my pleasure." The New makes him so dependent upon the volitions of moral agents, that he is liable to suffer disappointment, and to have his happiness diminished, by the uncontrollable agency of men:—and this not only in the present world, but in the next. Prof. Fitch affirms that God's "purpose was to confer on the beings composing his moral kingdom, the power of volition and choice, *and to use the best influence God could use on the whole to secure the holiness and prevent the sin of such beings, who themselves, and not he, were to have immediate power over their volitions.*" Again: "We affirm that the causes in *kind* which originate sin, being inseparably inherent in a moral universe, may so accumulate in DEGREE *under every system of pro-*

vidence and government which CAN *be pursued,* as to render sure the occurrence of sin. If in a universe of such beings, *no possible system of providence adopted and pursued* THROUGH ETERNITY *can shut out all occasions of the outbreakings of sin,* it is easy to see, that as to his preventing it, sin is unavoidably incidental to the acts of the Creator in creating and governing such a kingdom." . . . . . . "The causes in *kind* which are known to originate sin in the present universe, must necessarily be present in any possible universe of moral beings." . . . . . . "If the causes of defectibility are thus inseparable from the existence of a universe of moral beings, *is there not a ground of probability that they will lead to actual defection in every possible system as well as in this?*"—"Review of Dr. Fisk's Discourse on Predestination and Election, and a Defence of that Review in the Christian Spectator." What low and unworthy views does this statement convey concerning the Deity! What dismal prospects it presents to the expectant of future and eternal bliss!

2. The Old Theology regards the fall of man as a catastrophe so direful in its effects, that no power less than Omnipotence is adequate to "quicken sinners who are dead in trespasses and sins." The New treats it as a calamity, which the sinner is able, since the introduction of a system of mercy through Jesus Christ, to repair himself. Says Mr. Finney, "Now suppose God to have come out upon Adam with the command of the text, 'Make you a new heart, for why will ye die?' Could Adam have justly answered,

Dost thou think that I can change my own heart? Can I, who have a heart totally depraved, can I change that heart? Might not the Almighty have answered him in words of fire, Rebel, you have just changed your heart from holiness to sin, now change it back from sin to holiness."—*Sermons on Important Subjects*, p. 13. See also Mr. Barnes's remarks on the text, "When we were without strength, Christ died for the ungodly," in Chap. vii. We shall likewise give one or two additional quotations in the present chapter, under the head of Ability.

3. The Old Theology maintains that Adam was the federal head of his posterity, and that, by breaking the covenant under which he was placed, he involved not only himself, but all his posterity, in sin and misery—the guilt of his first sin being imputed to them, or set over in law to their account; so that they all come into the world with depraved and sinful natures. The New denies that we sustain a *covenant* relation to Adam; and maintains that he was only our *natural* head and father—from whose sin it results as a matter of fact, according to the common laws of human society, and that all his posterity become sinners when they arrive at moral agency; before which time they are neither sinful nor holy; and that they become sinners by their own *voluntary* act, after a trial, it would seem, similar to what Adam had. Says Dr. Taylor, in reply to a supposed objection, "Why render this universal sinfulness of a race, the consequence of one man's act? why not give to each a fair trial for himself?" "I answer, *God does give*

to each a fair trial for himself. Not a human being does or can become thus sinful or depraved but by his own choice. God does not compel him to sin by the *nature* he gives him. Nor is his sin, although a consequence of Adam's sin, in such a sense its consequence as not to be a free voluntary act of his own. He sins freely, voluntarily. There is no other way of sinning. God, (there is no irreverence in saying it,) can make nothing else sin but the sinner's act."—*Concio ad Clerum.*

Mr. Barnes observes: "If it were a dogma of a pretended revelation, that God might at pleasure, and by an arbitrary decree, make crime pass from one individual to another—striking onward from age to age, and reaching downward to 'the last season of recorded time'—punished in the original offender; repunished in his children; and punished again and again by infinite multiples, in countless ages and individuals; and all this judicial infliction, for a single act, performed cycles of ages before the individuals lived, we see not how any evidence could shake our intrinsic belief that this is unjust and improbable." . . . . . "We never can adopt that system which tramples on the analogies which actually exist, and holds men to be personally *answerable*, and actually *punished* by a just God, for an act committed thousands of years before they were born. Such a doctrine is no where to be found in the Scriptures."—*Introductory Essay to Butler's Analogy*, pp. 35, 39.

All that we deem it necessary to say concerning the views contained in these extracts, is, that *Uni-*

tarians consider them "*sound and lucid.*" In the Review of Mr. Barnes's Notes on the Romans, in the Christian Examiner, already referred to, [a Unitarian Quarterly] the reviewer says: "On the subject of man's nature, capacities, and duty, our author is *sound and lucid.* The idea of hereditary depravity he spurns, as unworthy of even a passing notice. He asserts repeatedly that men sin only *in their own person, in themselves,* as indeed how *can* they *sin* in any other way? The imputation of Adam's transgression he treats as a scholastic absurdity." . . . . "Of the figment of Adam's federal headship and the condemnation of his posterity for partnership in his sin, Mr. Barnes says 'there is not one word of it in the Bible.' "*

---

* The views of Socinus are as follows:

Quest. 1. "Is it in our power fully to obey the commandments of God?"

Answ. "Certainly; for it is evident, that the first man was so formed by God, that he was endued with free will; and no reason existed why he should be deprived of this power after the fall; nor was it consistent with the justice of God, that man should be deprived of free will. Accordingly, in the punishment inflicted on his sin, there is no mention made of any such loss."

Quest. 2. "But is not the will of man vitiated by original sin?"

Answ. "There is no such thing as original sin; the Scripture teaches no such doctrine; and the will of man could not be vitiated by a cause which had no existence. The sin of Adam, being a single act, could not corrupt his own nature, much less had it power to deprave the nature of all his posterity. That this sin should be charged on them, is, as has been

4. The Old Theology maintains that the atonement consisted in rendering satisfaction to divine justice by the vicarious sufferings of Christ, who endured in our stead the penalty of the law, and offered up himself an acceptable sacrifice to God: by which offering God's "favour was propitiated for us," his law magnified, and his government sustained: so that without doing violence to his holy nature, or relinquishing the claims of his law, or dishonouring his government, he *secured* the salvation of those who were given to Christ in the covenant of redemption; John xvii. 2; Isa. liii. 11, 12; and laid the foundation for a free *offer* of mercy to all who hear the gospel. Mark xvi. 15; John iii. 16.

The New Theology considers the atonement as involving a *suspension* of the penalty of the law, and as consisting in a "*symbolical display*" to the universe, for the purpose of producing such an impression of God's hatred to sin, as would render it safe and proper for him as moral Governor, to bestow pardon upon sinners: and as to sinners themselves, it is an "*experiment*," made by God for their salvation; which, through his impotency to control moral agents, may *fail* of its intended result.* Among

---

said, a doctrine unknown to the Scriptures; and it is utterly incredible, that God, who is the fountain of equity, should be willing to impute it to them."—*Racovian Catechism*, compiled from the writings of Socinus, and published A. D. 1606; translated for the Biblical Repertory; q. v.

* I have not met with any writer who expressed himself in this revolting form, except Mr. Jenkyn, in his work on the

other *relations* of the atonement discussed by Mr. Jenkyn, he considers it in relation to the *purposes* and *providences* of God. Under the former he observes, "The various dispensations of probation are various *experiments* in moral government, in which *God submits his own plans* and ways to the acceptance and for the use of *free agents*. If any object to the word '*experiment*,' I beg to refer them for the meaning of it, to the parable of the barren fig-tree, and to that of the husbandman sending his servants, and afterwards his son to the vineyard. These dispensations or *experiments* are capable of *failure*. The Eden *experiment failed*—and the Sinai *experiment failed*. Such susceptibility of *failure* has been shown to be *incidental to a moral government* and a state of trial." Under its relation to *providence* he says, "The measures of providence are liable to *failure*. A medicine may fail, notwithstanding the virtue which providence has given it. The crop of the husbandman may fail, notwithstanding the provision that seed-time and harvest-time shall continue. *The morbid fear of acknowledging such a liableness to failure in the measures of providence* is unaccountable, when *God declares his own government of the Jews, under the theocracy, to have failed of its end.* 'In vain have I smitten them, they have refused to

Atonement. But this is a correct statement, it appears to me, of the doctrine, as held by those (if they are consistent) who, in connection with the New-school view of atonement, adopt also the new theory concerning the character and government of God.

receive correction.' Jer. ii. 30. The word of God distinctly and expressly recognizes the same *liableness to failure in the great measure of atonement.* Are you sure that it is not attachment to system rather than attachment to the truth that makes you hesitate to avow it?" pp. 97, 168. Quere. If God's "*plan*" or "*experiment*," or "*measure of atonement*," is liable to *failure;* and if it *does fail* in numerous instances, as Mr. Jenkyn intimates, and elsewhere admits, what *security* have we that it will not *fail altogether?* What if it should happen, that when "*submitted to the acceptance of free agents*," they should *all* object to it, and refuse to comply with its conditions! Has God *power to control* the exercise of their *free agency* and *persuade* them to *change their minds?* or may they not, in despite of his mightiest influence, persist in rejecting Christ, and so despoil him of his mediatorial reward?

5. The Old Theology arrays the believer in the robe of Christ's righteousness; which being imputed to him and received by faith, is the ground of his justification before God. "This is his name whereby he shall be called, THE LORD OUR RIGHTEOUSNESS." Jer. xxiii. 6. "And be found in him, not having mine own righteousness, which is of the law, but that which is through the faith of Christ, the righteousness of God by faith." Phil. iii. 9. "And to her [the Lamb's wife, the church,] was granted, that she should be arrayed in fine linen, clean and white: for the fine linen is the righteousness of saints." Rev. xix. 8. "You have here," says Henry, "a descrip-

tion of the bride, how she appeared; *in fine linen, clean and white,* which is, *the righteousness of saints;* in the robes of *Christ's righteousness,* both *imputed* for justification, and *imparted* for sanctification."

The New Theology discards the doctrine of imputed righteousness, and maintains that the believer's *faith,* being an act which God approves, and which leads to other holy acts, is reckoned to him for righteousness; and in consequence of it God pardons his sin and receives him into favour. "Faith," says Mr. Finney, "is the appointed instrument of our justification, because it is the natural instrument of sanctification. It is the instrument of bringing us back to obedience, and therefore is designated as the means of obtaining the blessings of that return. It is not *imputed* to us by an arbitrary act, FOR what it is not, but *for what it is,* as the foundation of all real obedience to God. This is the reason why faith is made the medium through which pardon comes. It is simply set down to us for what it really is; because it first leads us to obey God from a principle of love to him."—*Lectures to Professing Christians,* p. 221.

Which of these doctrines is more calculated to humble the creature and to honour Christ? "If faith itself is our justifying righteousness, then it justifies as a work, as truly as any other works could; and" . . . . "if a man is justified on account of the act of believing, and that act he can perform by the power of free will, he has as much ground of boasting as he could possibly have, if he had been justified by other works."—*Dr. Alexander.*

6. The Old Theology places the sinner at the threshold of sovereign mercy, a *dependent* though guilty suppliant for grace and salvation. The New gives him sufficient ability to do all that God requires of him, without divine aid. In a review of Watson's Institutes in the *Christian Spectator*, are found the following: "He [Mr. Watson] repeatedly speaks of the power of the will, by which he intends, of course, its 'gracious ability' before the fall, as being lost by Adam, 'for himself and for his descendants.'" . . . . . "Admitting it to be true in Adam's case, that by sinning *he* was shorn of his power to obey God, what has this to do with his *posterity?* The principle assumed in the argument, renders it impossible, that their moral agency should be unhinged, until they exist and sin; therefore *Adam's sin could have no more tendency to destroy their power to choose good, or to set their teeth on edge, than it had to produce the same effects upon Satan and his apostate host.*" . . . . . . "We should like to know, whether the admirers of Mr. Watson believe it impossible for God to create a being, *possessing in himself the ability to choose good and be holy, without the gift of the Spirit?* and if so, where is his omnipotence? If it is admitted that he *can* create such a being, we ask whether the principles of divine government do not fully demonstrate, that *man is such a being?* If he is not, is God's government adapted to him? What notion can be formed of a subject of moral government, who is destitute of moral liberty? or in other words, who, in every instance of obedience or disobedience,

does not act with inherent power to the contrary choice?'"*—*Christian Spectator*, 1835, pp. 376, 377.

7. The Old Theology makes regeneration a *radical* change—a change in the *disposition* and *temper* of the sinner, as well as in his *acts*. The New regards it as merely giving a different *direction* to our constitutional desires; but appears to make little or no difference between the *principles* of action, in converted and unconverted men. They differ only as to the "*end* of pursuit." In reference to a sentiment advanced by Dr. Griffin, that the sinner has *no taste for holiness*, and therefore cannot be regenerated by *motives*, Mr. Gilbert remarks, "The impenitent sinner has no 'taste' for *conviction;* his unholy temper is as really opposed to *truth* as to *holiness;* and this philosophy would make it as impossible to *convict* as to convert him; to sanctify as to regenerate him. The unconverted man has no 'taste' for conviction, nor the converted man for *more* sanctification." Mark, "*The unconverted man has no taste for conviction, nor the converted man for* MORE *sanctification!*" What then is the difference between the *taste* or *temper*, or *disposition* of an impenitent sinner, and a child of God? For aught we can perceive, they are precisely the same.

8. The Old Theology gives honour to Christ and the Holy Spirit—the New has a tendency to throw them, particularly the latter, into the shade. "You

---

* Concerning the power of contrary choice, see Dr. Beecher's views, and Dr. Harvey's remarks upon them in Chapter vii.

see (says Mr. Finney) how unphilosophical it is, while pressing the sinner to submission, to divert his mind and turn his attention to the subject of the Spirit's influence. While his attention is directed to that subject, his submission is impossible." *Sermons on Important Subjects*, p. 61. Of course, those who would be instrumental in converting sinners, must say little or nothing about the Spirit.* And it is true, as a matter of *fact*, that the class of preachers

---

* I have in my possession a written statement communicated to me by a very respectable minister, which affords another illustration of this sentiment. Says he, "In the summer of 1832, while travelling in the valley of the Mississippi, I spent a few weeks in the city of ——, and gave assistance, as I was able, by request of the pastor in —— church of that place. Unusual attention to religion existed when I arrived, and continued for some time. A strong tendency was manifested both to new doctrines and new measures. One evening when on the way to the church with the pastor, where I had engaged to preach, *he requested I should say nothing in my preaching, concerning the influences of the Spirit*, as he had new views on repentance. He did not deny the work of the Spirit, but thought it should not be preached. He was then, and still remains a leading member of his Synod." To this we will add the following:

A former student of Dr. Taylor has informed me, verbally, that he heard Dr. Taylor advance the sentiment in two different sermons, "*that sinners must act in the work of conversion just as if there was no Holy Ghost.*" To prove the truth of his remark, he alluded to Acts xix. 2. "We have not so much as heard whether there be any Holy Ghost." He had heard, also, through others, of Dr. Taylor's advancing the same sentiment at different times; and he believed he was in the *habit* of doing it where he preached a course of revival sermons.

to which we now refer, say almost as little about *Christ* as about the Spirit. They preach much about *submitting to God;* but they seldom exhibit the second person of the Trinity, in his mediatorial character, and the duty of embracing him as a Saviour. The apostolic direction, "Believe in the Lord Jesus Christ," is exchanged for a phraseology which is calculated to convey the impression that conversion consists in the mere choice of God as a moral Governor. This indeed is Mr. Finney's account of it. "It [a change of heart] is a change in the choice of a *Supreme Ruler*." .... "The world is divided into two great political parties; the difference between them is, that one party choose Satan as the God of this world;" .... "the other party choose Jehovah for their Governor." Jesus Christ, as a distinct person in the Godhead, and faith in him as our Redeemer, appear to have little to do in the process.*

9. The Old Theology honours the Holy Scriptures, by drawing its doctrines and proofs from this source

---

* In the summer of 1834, I heard a sermon from Professor ———— of New Haven. I do not recollect that there was a sentiment in it to which I took exceptions; and yet there was such an *absence* of what a Christian desires and expects to find, in a sermon which professed to teach us how we may approach God with acceptance, as to afford too much reason for the observation of a pious and intelligent lady soon after, viz: "that he kept Christ and the Holy Spirit so much out of view, she could not help thinking that he was a deist." This lady had not yet heard the name or residence of the preacher; and of course could not have been influenced by any considerations of this kind.

alone, without calling in the aid of philosophy. The New resorts to the latter, in order to obtain its first principles; and then interprets the former so as to make them accord with these philosophical opinions. This remark, we are aware, may be called in question. The leaders in the New-school party have had much to say concerning the "*facts*" of Scripture, and have charged their brethren of the Old-school with resorting to philosophy. But a little investigation of this subject, will show the statement first made to be strictly true. In Mr. Finney's two sermons on the duty of sinners to change their own hearts, he uses the words philosophy, philosophical, unphilosophical, &c., at least fourteen times. He tells us about "the *philosophy* of conversion," "the *philosophy* of self-examination," and "the *philosophy* of special efforts to promote revivals of religion." Every step in the change is brought to the test of *philosophy:* and the failure of the sinner to submit to God is ascribed in one instance to his not understanding the *philosophy* of the process. "He, therefore, (says he) who does not understand the *philosophy* of this; who does not understand the use and power of *attention*, the use and power of conscience, and upon what to fix his mind, to lead him to a right decision, will naturally complain that he does not know how to submit." The Scriptures are also brought forward and compared by this rule. "When he [Joshua] assembled the people of Israel and laid their duty before them, and said, 'choose you this day whom ye will serve,' he did not *unphilosophically* remind them at the same time of their dependence upon the Spirit of God." Thus we have *philosophical* preaching, *philosophical* protracted meetings, *philosophical* self-examination, *philosophical* submission, and *philosophical* conversion. May not the result of the whole be a merely *philosophical christian?* Other proofs which might be adduced, from different writers, we must leave to those who desire to examine this subject.

It may possibly be said that we have given more prominence to Mr. Finney than was proper; since he goes further than most of his brethren, and is not, therefore, a fair specimen of their views. We admit he has expressed himself more *freely* than perhaps *any* one else; but if we compare the quotations made from various authors, we shall perceive they all belong to the same family. It has been our aim both in our statements and quotations, to exhibit the doctrines of the New Theology, just as they are, without the least exaggeration. For this purpose our extracts from New-school authors have been numerous, and sufficiently extended as to length, to give a correct view of their sentiments.* But if it can be made to appear that we have misrepresented their views in a single important point, we shall cheerfully rectify the mistake.

* In the succeeding chapters, not found in the first two editions, additional facts are given touching their views—also other important matters.

PERFECTIONISM OF MR. FINNEY.

THERE is one extreme into which Mr. Finney has fallen, that we by no means charge upon the New School, as a body—and we have therefore as yet entirely omitted it. We mean his *perfectionism*. In this we presume he has few followers. We will however bestow upon it a little attention, that it may serve as a beacon to admonish those who have embarked on the voyage of religious discovery.

In his Lectures to professing Christians, he has two on Christian Perfection; and he adverts to the subject in several others. He defines perfection in the following words: "It is to love the Lord our God with all our heart and soul and mind and strength, and to love our neighbour as ourselves." This he maintains is attainable in the present life. "1. God wills it. 2. *All the promises and prophecies of God* that respect the sanctification of believers in this world, are to be understood of course *of their perfect sanctification.* 3. Perfect sanctification is *the great blessing* promised throughout the Bible. 4. The perfect sanctification of believers is the very *object for which the Holy Spirit is promised.* 5. If it is not a practicable duty to be perfectly holy in this world, then it will follow that the devil has so completely accomplished his design in corrupting mankind, that Jesus Christ is at a fault, and has *no way to sanctify his people, but to take them out of the world.* 6. If perfect sanctification is not attainable in this world, it must be, either from a want of motives in the gospel, or a want of sufficient power in the Spirit of God."

In another lecture he appears to teach perfection in *knowledge* as well as in holiness; amounting to an illumination little short of divine inspiration. " *The manner* in which the Spirit of God does this," says he, *i. e.* communicates ideas to the mind without the use of words, "is what we can never know in this world. But the fact is undeniable, that he can reach the mind without the use of words, and can put our minds in possession of the ideas themselves, of which the types, or figures, or words, of the human teacher, are only the signs or imperfect representatives." . . . . "The needed influences of the Spirit of God may be possessed by all men freely under the gospel." . . . . . " They [ministers] should not attempt to explain passages of which they are not confident *they have been taught the meaning by the Holy Spirit.* It is presumption. And they need not do it, for they may always have the teachings of the Spirit by asking." . . . . . . " This is applicable both to preachers and to teachers in Sabbath schools and Bible classes." . . . . . . "Will you lay your hearts open to God, and not give him rest, *till he has filled you with divine knowledge?*"

In other lectures he goes further still, and maintains, if I understand his language, that when the Christian has thus given himself up entirely to Christ, to be taught and governed by him, he becomes so identified with Christ, that his spirit and Christ's Spirit are, morally considered, *one*—Christ becomes responsible for his acts; and of course he not only ceases from sin, but he *cannot* commit sin. Whatever he does, Christ is responsible for it. This he calls entering into rest. "When one ceases from his own works, he so perfectly gives up his own interest and his own will, and places himself so perfectly under the dominion and guidance of the Holy Spirit, that whatever he does is done by the impulse of the Spirit of God." . . . . . "They are in one sense our works, because we do them by our voluntary agency. Yet in another sense they are his works, because he is the moving cause of all." . . . . . . "He [Christ] is just as absolutely your sanctification, as your justification. If you depend upon him for sanctification, he will no more let you sin than he will let you go to hell." . . . . "The reputation of the wife is wholly united to that of her husband, so that his reputation is hers, and her reputation is his. What affects her character affects his; and what affects his character affects hers. Their reputation is one, their interests are one. So with the church; whatever concerns the church is just as much the interest of Christ, as if it was personally his own matter." . . . . "If any actions or civil liability come against the wife, the husband is responsible. If the wife has committed a trespass, the husband is answerable. It is his business to guide and govern her, and her business to obey, and if he does not restrain her from breaking the laws, he is responsible." . . . . . "In like manner, Jesus Christ is Lord

over his church, and if he does not actually restrain his church from sin, he has it to answer for." ......
"It is his business to take care of the church, and control her, and keep her from sin; and for every sin of every member, Jesus Christ is responsible, and must answer." ...... "O! if believers would only throw themselves wholly on Christ, and make him responsible, by placing themselves entirely at his control, they would know his power to save, and would live without sin."

We have given these extracts at some length, that those who have not access to his Lectures, may obtain a full view of his sentiments. It is scarcely necessary to remark, that the sentences last quoted are *Antinomian*. The history of Antinomianism does not furnish many expressions, more licentious in their tendency than these. This heresy is more frequently the result of an *abuse* of the doctrines of grace; but in the present instance, it appears to have originated in an opposite cause, viz: in those views of human ability, which render grace in a measure superfluous.* "There is," says he, "no more moral

---

* It is supposed by some that there is no logical connection between Mr. Finney's former and present views—but that he has got upon a new track. Formerly, as one observes, "he left Christ and the Holy Spirit almost out of view; he hardly preached the gospel at all; but now Christ and the Holy Spirit are every thing. He pushes union with Christ, imputation, covenant relation, &c., into Antinomianism." The only connection, he says, between the latter and his Pelagianism, is that he "is a fanatic now as he was before." But as others think differently, we shall state the probable process by which

inability to be *perfectly* holy, than there is to be holy at all." On the same principle, therefore, that he could preach to the sinner the practicability of changing his own heart, he might argue that the Christian can arrive at perfect holiness in this life. He actually adopts the same mode of reasoning in both cases. It is therefore very natural to conclude, that the frequent discussion of the subject of ability in reference to the sinner, had much to do in forming his opinions with regard to Christian perfection. Having arrived at this point, he applied his ideas of perfection, not only to our sanctification, but to all our relations to God. In a lecture from the text, "Who of God is made unto us wisdom, and righteousness, and sanctification, and redemption;" he considers each of the terms as conveying an idea equally expressive. Since then, according to the views which he had previously adopted, sanctification was to be taken as implying *perfect* holiness, the perfectibility of wisdom would seem to follow as a consequence. Hence he says in regard to this, "As he [Christ] is the infinite source of wisdom, how can it be said that he is made unto us wisdom, unless we are partakers of his wisdom, and have it guarantied to us; so that, at any time, if we trust in him, we may have it as certainly, and in any degree we need, to guide us as infallibly, as if we had

it is supposed he was led into these errors. Yet whether they are the "logical sequence" of his former views or not, they furnish an instructive lesson to those who are disposed to countenance error.

it originally ourselves?" Thus we are brought into the field of fanaticism.

The only condition required in order to obtain either wisdom or sanctification, is faith. "The act of the mind, says he, that thus throws the soul into the hand of Christ for sanctification, is faith. Nothing is wanting, but for the mind to break off from any confidence in itself, and to give itself up to him, to be led and controlled by him absolutely." Then Christ asumes the responsibility; he undertakes to do all for him that he needs; he becomes accountable for his conduct. Says he, "Until an individual receives Christ, he does not cease from his own works. The moment he does that, by this very act he throws the entire responsibility upon Christ. The moment the mind does fairly yield itself up to Christ, the responsibility comes upon him, just as the person who undertakes to conduct the blind man is responsible for his safe conduct. The believer by the act of faith pledges Christ for his obedience and sanctification. By giving himself up to Christ, all the veracity of the Godhead is put at stake, that he shall be led aright, or made holy." Here we have the final result of the whole process. By the proper exercise of our free will, we can first change our own hearts, or in other words, put forth the "act" of saving faith upon Jesus Christ. By the proper exercise of the same free will, we can put forth a stronger "act" of faith, and make him our wisdom and sanctification:—our wisdom, in such a sense, that he will "guide us infallibly, as if we had it originally ourselves:"—and our sanctification, so entire and absolute, that Christ becomes responsible for our conduct, and "if he does not restrain us from sin, he has it to answer for."

In the March number of the Literary and Theological Review for the year 1838, there is an able article on this subject, from which we will make the following extract. "In the works before us [referring to Mr. Finney's Sermons and Lectures,] we have an authentic genealogy of a *family of errors.* We are not obliged, as in other instances, to trace them through successive generations of men. They are all found in the same mind, and *Pelagianism,* as contained in the preceding extracts, is the venerable ancestor of them all. From his infancy it was remarked that he was an *uncommon child.* Unlike other children, he was by nature neither '*sinful nor holy.*' Unhappily, however, very soon after his birth, he '*fell into a state of supreme selfishness,*' from which even the 'physical power of God' could not extricate him. But he had *rare abilities,* and a 'giant strength' of will, which he could hardly refrain from calling '*the strength of Omnipotence.*' And therefore, he always believed himself to be one of those who could be recovered '*with the wisest amount of moral influence.*' He had elevated notions of human virtue, and would suffer no change to be made in his condition, which was not produced by '*his own act.*' He was willing, indeed, that the Holy Spirit should operate on him, provided it were only *as an earthly advocate acts on a jury.* He was willing that '*motives should be gathered from all worlds and.*

poured in a focal blaze on his mind.' He was anxious to receive good counsel from his friends, and reverently to hear divine truth; but the change from '*supreme selfishness*' he declared to be his own '*appropriate work;*' and he was at length accustomed to say, that he had effected it by '*his own act.*' It was natural to suppose, that the theological children of such a system would have some remarkable characteristics. In Pelagius and Cœlestius it had produced Perfectionism, and there was reason to fear that in the mind of Mr. Finney it would generate the same progeny. In various parts of the land the system had been earnestly inculcated. Its most sagacious disciples were beginning to declare themselves to '*be perfect,*' to have '*rolled the responsibility of their future and eternal obedience on an everlasting arm;*' to receive '*immediate communications from God;*' to be '*personally united to him,*' and have '*entered into rest.*' "

These heresies were early demonstrated to have had their origin in the system itself. As Mr. Finney had been the Apostle of this system in these latter days, it was intimated that his doctrines, as inculcated in his preaching and by the press, had tended to produce these impieties. This view of the subject was indignantly repelled even by the candid ones among his followers. The thought that *his doctrines* had produced such results, they could not for a moment entertain. Although others had no doubt that Mr. Finney was the true parent of Perfectionism, they had more opinion of his caution, than to suppose he could soon be induced openly to own and adopt it. But, to the amazement of all, he now comes forth, bringing with him for induction into the church, the doctrine of *the perfection of the saints in this life, of the responsibility of Christ for his people, of immediate communications to them from God, and of their entrance into rest even in this world.* These last views were not developed till he had abandoned the Presbyterian Church. Ever since their publication, it is almost inconceivable by those who have heard of him chiefly as a promoter of revivals, and have been unwilling to listen to the notes of warning, so long honestly and responsively sounded by *individuals*—it is almost inconceivable, that he has inculcated these fanatical doctrines. Even the Christian Spectator, though it fears " he may be liable to misconstruction, and injure the consciences of many weak and pious persons," declares, " we do not believe he means any thing more than we should fully admit—the possibility and duty of obedience to God in all things commanded." But this view of his meaning it is impossible to sustain, either by individual sentences, or the evident design of his Lectures on these subjects. His errors are written so legibly, that he who runs may read. Mr. Finney now stands before the community as a practical illustration of the effects of rejecting the doctrine, that *human nature is depraved:* and of believing, that in regeneration and sanctification, *the word of the Spirit is confined chiefly to the understanding.*

CHAPTER X.

THE MEASURES ADOPTED BY THE GENERAL ASSEMBLY FOR REMOVING THESE ERRORS FROM THE PRESBYTERIAN CHURCH.

ON the supposition that the errors specified in the preceding chapters were prevalent in any portion of the Presbyterian Church, it is no wonder that many should feel alarmed. Some of these doctrines had been made the ground of discipline at different times before this period. In 1798, the case of Rev. H. Balch came before the Assembly, by way of reference from the Synod of the Carolinas. The following is a part of the minutes of the Assembly on this subject: "With regard to his doctrine of original sin, it is to be observed, that he is erroneous in representing personal corruption as not derived from Adam; making Adam's sin to be imputed to his posterity, in consequence of a corrupt nature *already possessed,* and derived from, we know not what; thus in effect setting aside the idea of Adam's being the federal head, or representative, of his descendants, and the whole doctrine of the covenant of works."

"It is also manifest that Mr. B. is greatly erroneous, in asserting that the formal cause of a believer's justification is the imputation of the *fruits and effects* of Christ's righteousness, and not that righteousness itself; because righteousness, and that alone, is the formal demand of the law, and consequently the sinner's violation of the divine law can be pardoned only by virtue of the Redeemer's perfect righteousness being imputed to him and reckoned as his. It is also not true that the *benefits* of Christ's righteousness are, with strict propriety, said to be *imputed* at all, as these benefits *flow to*, and are *possessed by*, the believer, as a *consequence* of his justification and having an interest in the infinite merits of the Saviour."

In 1810, a work of the Rev. William C. Davis, entitled the "Gospel Plan," came before the Assembly, by an overture from the Synod of the Carolinas. Among the doctrines contained in the book, of an exceptionable character, and which the Assembly condemned, are the following: "That the active obedience of Christ constitutes no part of that righteousness by which a sinner is justified;" that "God could not make Adam, or any other creature, either holy or unholy;" and that "if God has to plant all the principal parts of salvation in a sinner's heart, to enable him to believe, the gospel plan is quite out of his reach, and consequently does not suit his case; and it must be impossible for God to condemn a man for unbelief, for no just law condemns or criminates any person for not doing what he cannot do." Concerning these doctrines the Assembly resolved that they are "contrary to the Confession of Faith of our church."—*Assembly's Digest*, pp. 130, 145, 146, 147.

The first of these cases was adjudicated ten years, and the second twenty-two years, after the organization of the General Assembly; and they show that for twenty-two years after that event, those doctrines which led to the division of the church in 1837, were regarded and treated as heretical and dangerous. They serve also as a key to the received interpretation of the Confession of Faith prior to that period, and to the proper understanding of the famous "Adopting Act" of 1729.

CHARACTER OF THE ADOPTING ACT.

The act denominated the "Adopting Act," which was unanimously agreed to by the Synod of Philadelphia, in 1729, required "that all the ministers of this Synod, or that shall hereafter be admitted to this Synod, shall declare their agreement in and approbation of the Confession of Faith, with the Larger and Shorter Catechisms of the Assembly of Divines at Westminster, as being, in all essential and necessary articles, good forms and sound words, and systems of Christian doctrine; and [we] do also adopt the said Confession of Faith and Catechisms as the confession of our faith. And we do also agree that the Presbyteries within our bounds shall always take care not to admit any candidate for the ministry into the exercise of the sacred functions, but what declares his agreement in opinion with all essential and necessary articles of said Confession, either by subscribing the said Confession of Faith and Catechisms, or by verbal declaration of his assent thereto, as such minister or candidate shall think best. And in case any minister of this Synod, or any candidate for the ministry, shall have any scruples with regard to any article or articles of said Confession of Faith or Catechisms, he shall, at the time of his making such declaration, declare his sentiments to the Presbytery or Synod, who shall, notwithstanding, admit him to the exercise of the ministry within our bounds, and to ministerial communion, if either the Presbytery or Synod shall judge his scruples or mistakes to be only about articles not essential and necessary in doctrine, worship, or government."

This provision appears to be understood by some of our New-school brethren as giving so wide a latitude for diversity of sentiment, that, in their opinion, it was only by a departure from the design and spirit of that instrument, and the introduction into the church of a narrow and intolerant spirit, that the new theology was not allowed to remain quietly, and spread itself throughout our bounds. How utterly unfounded this opinion is, will appear from the manner in which the Synod carried the "Adopting Act" into effect. On the same day in which it was passed, all the ministers present, except one who was not then prepared, but who subsequently acceded to the resolution, "after proposing all the scruples that any of them had to make against any articles and expressions in the Confession of Faith, and Larger and Shorter Catechisms of the Assembly of Divines at Westminster, unanimously agreed in the solution of those scruples, and in declaring the said Confession and Catechisms to be the confession of their faith, excepting only some clauses in the twentieth and twenty-third chapters, concerning which clauses the Synod unanimously declared that they did not receive those articles in any such sense as to suppose the civil magistrate hath a controlling power over Synods, with respect to the exercise of their ministerial authority, or power to persecute any for their religion, or in any sense contrary to the Protestant succession to the throne of Great Britain."

The following year, and again in 1736, the Synod adopted a resolution explanatory of their former action. In the latter they say, "that the Synod have adopted and still do adhere to the Westminster Confession, Catechisms, and Directory, without the least variation or alteration." . . . . . . "And we do further declare this was our meaning and true intent in our first adopting of the said Confession."

In 1741 a schism took place, by which two Synods were formed, and an unhappy alienation existed between them for seventeen years. During this separation both parties adopted resolutions to the effect that they adhered "to the Westminster Confession of Faith, Catechisms, and Directory, without the least variation or alteration," agreeably to the action of the Synod in 1729—and neither party charged the other with practising or desiring any unwarranted latitude of interpretation. The division did not originate in doctrinal differences. Hence, when the overture was made for a re-union, the Synod of New York say to the Synod of Philadelphia, "We esteem mutual forbearance a duty, since we all profess the same Confession of Faith and Directory." The latter Synod, in reply to the former, employed similar language. "Upon these terms (viz. the terms specified in their letter) we heartily agree with the Synod of New York, that since we profess the same Confession of Faith and Directory for worship, all our former differences be buried in perpetual oblivion." Accordingly, one of the terms of union unanimously adopted by the two bodies was the following: "Both Synods having always approved and received the Westminster Confession of Faith, Larger and Shorter Catechisms, as an orthodox and excellent system of Christian doctrine, founded upon the word of God, we do still receive the same as the confession of our faith, and also adhere to the plan of worship, government, and discipline, contained in the Westminster Directory: strictly enjoining it on all our ministers and probationers for the ministry, that they preach and teach according to the form of sound words in the said Confession and Catechisms, and avoid and oppose all errors contrary thereto."

In 1786, two years before the organization of the General Assembly, a plan of union was proposed between the Presbyterian, Dutch, and Associate Reformed Churches. The committee on the part of the Synod of New York and Philadelphia, were instructed to say, that the Synod " adopt, according to the known and established meaning of terms, the Westminster Confession of Faith as the confession of their faith, save that every candidate for the gospel ministry is permitted to except against so much of the twenty-third chapter as gives authority to the civil magistrate in matters of religion." For a full account of the Adopting Act, see *Hodge's Constitutional History of the Presbyterian Church*, Vol. i., Chap. iii.

From these several particulars, it is very evident

that the liberty granted in the Adopting Act, to any minister or candidate, to state his "scruples with regard to any article or articles of the Confession of Faith and Catechisms," and that he should be admitted "to the exercise of the ministry," if either the Presbytery or Synod shall judge his scruples or mistakes to be only about articles *not essential and necessary* in doctrine, worship, or government," was restricted practically to a very few things; and that with regard to these and all others, the scruples of the minister or candidate were not be confined to his own breast, nor even stated in general terms, but particularized before the Presbytery or Synod; and that his brethren were to judge, not the applicant himself, whether his scruples or mistakes were a valid bar to his reception as a member. How widely different from this, is that mode of assenting to the Confession of Faith, which professes to receive it only for "substance of doctrine," and which requires of the candidate no statement of his "scruples" to the Presbytery, but leaves it wholly to his own decision whether they are such as are "essential and necessary," or otherwise. It is evident, from the cases adjudicated by the Assembly in 1798 and 1810, already referred to, that that body did not so understand the "Adopting Act," as to allow this mode of receiving the Confession of Faith, nor interpret it in such a manner as to permit the new theology to exist in the church without censure. They arraigned and condemned some of those very errors which have been enumerated in the preceding chapters—and in doing this they did not depart in the least from the provisions of the "Adopting Act," nor from the views expressed concerning it by successive Synods, up to the time of the formation of the General Assembly—but were carrying out those views in the way which had been definitely stipulated and agreed to, by the articles of union between the Synods of New York and Philadelphia, in 1758, viz: "strictly enjoining it on all their ministers and probationers for the ministry, that they preach and teach according to the form of sound words in the said Confession and Catechisms, and avoid and oppose all errors contrary thereto."

PREVALENCE OF ERRORS.

The question now arises, did those errors prevail in the bounds of the Presbyterian Church for some years prior to 1837? and if so, to what extent? The answer is found partly in the statements contained in the preceding chapters. But as the action of the Assembly, at that time, was directed chiefly towards the three Synods of Western New York, and the Synod of the Western Reserve, it will be proper to state some facts with special reference to them.

At the Auburn Convention, in 1837, (composed of ministers and elders called together to consider the Assembly's acts,) a distinguished member observed, that "he must say there had been hitherto a disposition to conceal; that errors and irregularities in this section of the church have been greater than we have been willing to acknowledge." At the same meeting the committee on doctrines reported a paper similar in its statements to one agreed upon in 1797, by a committee of the Presbyterian, Reformed Dutch, and Associate Reformed Churches, as the basis of an agreement for uniting in sending missionaries to the new settlements; accompanied by a list of errors, the same as those specified by the preceding General Assembly. One member proposed, as a substitute for the paper, the protest of the minority of the preceding Assembly. A second did not think that some of the errors there specified were fundamental, and he could not, therefore, solemnly pledge himself (as the report recommended) to discipline those whom he might know to hold them. A third said, he was persuaded that the Convention could not agree, either in the statement of doctrine in detail made in the report of the committee, or in that of the protestants in the last Assembly. A fourth expressed his concurrence with the one last referred to, and proposed that they should adopt the first part of the report of the committee without going into detail; which was accordingly done.

During the discussion of the above report, a prominent elder objected to the report, because some of the errors there specified he did not consider to be errors—for example, he did not believe that Adam's sin was imputed to his posterity. He was satisfied they never could agree on any creed as extensive as this; while we agree in substantials, we cannot agree in minor points; here every man must be allowed to have his own creed. This is the fault of our Confession of Faith—it is too extensive for agreement. State a few general points involving that we are sinners and are saved by the grace of God, through Jesus Christ and the agency of the Holy Ghost, and we can agree; but when you come to speak of the *quo modo* we cannot be expected to agree. We have a right to differ; if we agree on these points, woe to him who pronounces such men heretics—we must have the right of private judgment. There are two opposite doctrines in the church; I can agree to receive as Christians those who hold to either, and sit under their ministry, though I differ from some of them. There are some who hold that we are born sinners before we arrive at moral agency; and they carry out the system to Antinomianism. Others hold God to be a moral governor, who governs man in a manner analogous to what is done in other governments. They are both *substantially* true—both contain the gospel, yet they are opposite."

Another member of the Convention (a minister) observed to me, in private conversation, "We are so trammelled and shackled, and under tyranny by Confessions of Faith, that if we advance any thing new, we are suspected of heresy. We ought to be making improvements in theology as much as in other matters." While, therefore, he would have a Confession of Faith, it should not be a permanent and fixed one, but subject to be modified with every additional light that should be thrown on the subject. Every minister, every church, and every Presbytery, should write a new confession of faith as often as once a year, and then, by comparing it with the old, see what changes (if any) were necessary to be made. I asked him whether he would not recommend the same course to the General Assembly, and have our Confession of Faith undergo a revision. He said he thought it ought to be altered in a number of particulars. I asked him how he could adopt it while entertaining such views. He replied, "I adopt it only as a *system*, without intending to subscribe to the whole of it. As a *system* I believe it; and provided I hold doctrines belonging *peculiarly to another* system—such as Arminian or Pelagian—I could not consistently, I confess, adopt the Confession, unless I stated my exceptions at the time of adopting it. When I first adopted it, I entertained different views on several points from what I do now, viz: atonement, the moral government of God, imputation, and original sin—but I believe I am as near the Confession now as I was then. I believe *substantially* as I did then, and I suppose that all the changes which might be required from time to time, with the addition of new light, would not alter it so as to make it *another system*. When it was written, a different philosophy prevailed from what does now—a false philosophy—through which some expressions were introduced into the Confession which are not true—*e. g.* 'sinned in him and fell with him in his first transgression'—which conveys a false idea." Do you mean, said I, that it contains a false idea, as the framers of the Confession understood it? "Yes, he said, as they understood it. Their philosophy was false—they held that we were really there in the garden, and partook of the forbidden fruit; he would, therefore, have this clause altered so as to make it accord with modern philosophy.* On the subject of God's moral government, he thought the Confession defective—he would have a whole chapter added on this subject." This is a specimen of a conversation which was continued in a similar strain for half an hour.

After these statements the reader will not be surprised that the report of the committee on doctrine was amended, by expunging from it "all the details" both of what the Convention believed, and what they regarded as errors. The paper as adopted was good as far as it went, but it was brief, and expressed in general terms. Some of the members would have been glad to adopt the report without alteration or abridgment, but they were overruled by others who thought differently. How many of them actually entertained the views narrated above, I cannot say;

---

* A similar caricature of Old-school views has been recently put forth, in a volume published by a committee of the Synod of New York and New Jersey. "Some of them believe in the identity of the posterity of Adam with him in his first transgression; others, that there was a literal transfer of his sin to them, as also of the righteousness of Christ to his people." We presume it will not be pretended that any portion of the church since the beginning of the present century, have gone further in maintaining these phases of doctrine than was done previous to that time. In the case adjudicated by the General Assembly in 1798, already noticed in this chapter, the Assembly say, "that the transferring of personal sin or righteousness has never been held by Calvinistic divines, nor by any person in our church, as far as is known to us."

but I have reason for believing that those two were not the only ones—and also that there were ministers and laymen in considerable numbers, belonging to those Synods, but not present at the Convention, whose theology was of the same stamp. In a letter, understood to have been written by a member of the Synod of Geneva, and published in the *Hartford Christian Watchman*, soon after the meeting of the General Assembly in 1837, the writer states: "I declared more than once before the Assembly, that the errors against which the Convention testified, do exist"—meaning the Convention which had been sitting for several days previous in Philadelphia. Another minister belonging to that Synod, wrote the same year to the author of this volume: "A considerable number of members, and two *ministers* (alluding to his own Presbytery), incline strongly to Taylorism—I should say are Taylorites—*more* are not sound Calvinists of the Edwards stamp. Our theology has many shades." From personal intercourse with different ministers in the Synod of Utica, and from other reliable testimony, I am warranted in saying that *some* of the ministers in each of the Presbyteries connected with that Synod, from 1830 to 1837, embraced the New Haven Theology; and that it prevailed to a considerable extent in their churches. A letter now in my possession, written by one of their ministers in 1833, to a clerical friend, contains the following: "O my dear brother, beware of that doctrine of a limited atonement. I hope I do not go too far, when I say it had its rise from the devil." . . .

... "It is astonishing, that at the present day of light and knowledge, men's understandings should be so blinded. For my part, I am awfully prejudiced against the Old-school divinity." ...... "I want you candidly to answer the following questions. Do you believe infants have a moral character? Are we to be accountable for the moral act of our first parents? What do you think of the New Haven Theology? Do you acquiesce in Dr. Taylor's notions? Do you consider them agreeable with the Scriptures? *His divinity is spreading very widely.*" .... "I am really glad that ——— has commenced his studies." .... "I hope he will not imbibe the principles of the Princeton Divinity."

A minister in the Synod of Genessee, in a letter penned in 1837, wrote thus: "Ministers and churches in this section have become so much disposed to favour Arminian doctrines, and are so fond of new things, that it is difficult to preach the doctrine of our Confession, or even to use our endeavours to correct abuses and extravagances in measures, without hearing the cry of Old-school, opposed to revivals," &c. Another minister wrote as follows: "New Theology and new measures have received a number of checks in our Presbytery, and, indeed, in this region generally—especially since the Old-school in the Assembly began to be so earnest for reform. Though I do not by any means suppose but what the *roots* of the evil remain among us yet, ready to spring up when permitted. Indeed, in one sense, almost the entire theology of this whole region is "*New,*" if strictly compared with our standards." At a protracted meeting in one of their churches in May, 1837, the officiating minister, after preaching a sermon on the ability of Christians to keep the law of God, called upon them to confess their sins, and promise to keep the law. Most of them were willing to confess, but when they came to make promises, there was a reluctance; as but few were prepared to fall in practically with the doctrine of the sermon. Some said, We will *try*—others, We will *endeavour by God's assistance*, &c.; but this did not satisfy him—he called it Antinomianism—and told them he wished them to promise, not that they would *try* to keep the law, but that they would *keep* it. A spice of perfectionism existed at that time in several of their churches, and also in some churches belonging to the Synods before named—but it was discountenanced, and made a ground of discipline by some of the Presbyteries, perhaps by all where it was known to exist. The same cannot be stated concerning the Synod of the Western Reserve, a majority of whose ministers and churches, we have reason to believe, accorded in doctrine with Mr. Finney. This is inferred concerning the ministers, from the fact, that in 1834 or 1835, a paper was signed by fifty ministers or more, inviting Mr. Finney to become Professor of Theology in the Western Reserve College; and concerning ministers and people both, it may be inferred from the fact that the labours of Mr. Foote, as an evangelist, (who preached extensively among them) were generally approved. Mr. Foote, it was understood, agreed substantially with Mr. Finney, but went further than the latter in some points, from what is called Old-school theology.

ATTEMPTS TO CHECK THESE ERRORS.

Attempts were made to check these errors as early as 1829 or 1830, and were continued every year till the occurrence of those decisive measures adopted by the Assembly in 1837. Individual efforts were made through the press, by the publication of books, pamphlets, and periodicals. Besides the able Quarterly at Princeton, which had been commenced a little previous, and a monthly Magazine at Philadelphia, both of which did good service in defence of the truth, four weekly newspapers were either established or resuscitated for the special purpose of counteracting these errors, and those "new measures" which were generally associated with them—one in Utica, a second in Albany, a third in Philadelphia, and a fourth in Pittsburgh. The last two have been continued to this day. Prosecutions for heresy were instituted in two instances, against distinguished individuals before their Presbyteries, on the charge of holding and teaching some of those errors. The Board of Missions refused to commission men as missionaries, who were suspected of entertaining those views. The gratuitous distribution of the Confession of Faith "among the more remote and destitute churches," was provided for by vote of the Assembly. That body enjoined on Presbyteries to take special care to require of candidates for licensure and ordination, and of ministers entering our Church from other ecclesiastical connections, to give their assent to the "Constitution of the Presbyterian Church;" and a paper was adopted by the Assembly to the effect, that an assent to this constitution had always been considered as a reception and adoption of the Westminster Confession of Faith, and Larger and Shorter Catechisms as the confession of our faith. Particular attention was directed to operation of the Plan of Union of 1801, between Presbyterians and Congregationalists; and the Synod of the Western Reserve was especially directed to examine the state of the churches under its care, with reference to alleged departures from the Constitution of the Church, in ordaining ministers and receiving them from other churches "without being required by the Presbyteries to receive and adopt the Confession of Faith of the Presbyterian Church." (See *Minutes of Assembly* for 1832 and 1833.) Appeals from lower judicatories were also brought before the Assembly, containing charges of doctrinal error, and efforts were made (though unsuccessful) to secure the suspension of the persons on trial, from the office of the ministry.—*Minutes of the Assembly for* 1836.

The inefficiency of these measures was owing to several causes. One was, the earnest desire for peace, which induced many sound men to favour a conciliatory and compromising policy, so long as there was in their judgment any reasonable hope that the evils complained of would gradually cure themselves, without a resort to extreme measures.

A second was the effect of the Plan of Union to introduce into our body many ministers who regarded themselves as having a right under the provisions of that Plan, to receive our Confession of Faith only for substance of doctrine: and being men of *loose* doctrinal views (in the strict Presbyterian sense of this term) they were opposed to the exercise of discipline for doctrinal errors. By the operation of the same Plan (though by its perversion) hundreds of Congregational and mixed churches, claimed the right of being represented in our Presbyteries, Synods, and General Assembly, by men who were not ruling elders, and had never assented to, and did not profess to receive (except in the largest sense) the Presbyterian Confession of Faith. A third was the influence of the Home Missionary and American Education Societies, particularly the former, in introducing into our pulpits unsound men, who in some localities became so numerous as to form majorities in our church courts. These last two points may require some illustration.

OPERATION OF THE PLAN OF UNION.

As the Plan of Union permitted churches formed under it to enjoy their preferences either to be organized as Presbyterian or Congregational churches, or to be a mixture of the two, as circumstances might seem to render expedient; and as a large portion of the material for the churches in Western New York and Northern Ohio, called the Western Reserve, was composed of immigrants from New

England, where most of the churches were Congregational, it was to be expected that there would exist very extensively a partiality for the Congregational form of government. Hence it is not surprizing that in 1837 about one half of the churches in those Synods, taken as a whole, were Congregational, and that portions of many others preferred that kind of organization—some of them to such a degree as to be quite restive under the government of a church session. In the Synod of Utica the churches were about equally divided with respect to organization; in the Synods of Geneva and Genessee, about two-thirds were nominally Presbyterian, and in the Synod of the Western Reserve about three fourths were Congregational. In all of them, though there was an understanding that as churches they received in a very general manner the Confession of Faith of the Presbyterian Church, there was no formal adoption of it by the churches even as a "system" or for "substance of doctrine." The Assembly's Shorter Catechism was understood to be an epitome of the Presbyterian Confession of Faith, and that Catechism was held in high estimation in the New England churches, and hence those who left them and settled in Western New York and the Western Reserve felt no objection on doctrinal grounds to be connected with the Presbyterian body. Yet they did not feel themselves committed even to the Catechism, as their confession of faith. Each church had its own confession, and this might be enlarged or abbreviated, changed or modified, at the pleasure of the communicants. Through the influence of those evangelists called "revival men," who laboured extensively among them for eight or ten years, commencing in 1826, many of these confessions were altered, some in one way and some in another, so as to meet (in the judgment of their advisers) the demands of Christian charity, or to keep pace with the increasing light of the age. I state these facts, not conjecturally, but from the most reliable testimony. Many of their ministers were also from New England, and professed to receive the Confession of Faith only as a "system;" while some of them entered the Presbyterian Church without any formal adoption of our Standards. This is admitted by the Synod of the Western Reserve in its communication to the General Assembly in 1833. (See *Assembly's Minutes* for that year.) From these facts it is manifest, that in a Presbytery or Synod composed largely of such men, there would exist but little disposition to call any of its members to account for a departure from our Confession of Faith;—and that should they be admitted to seats in the General Assembly, they might be expected to oppose any measure brought forward in that body, having in view the prosecution either of ministers or churches for doctrinal error.

THE AMERICAN EDUCATION AND HOME MISSIONARY SOCIETIES.

The injurious influence of the American Education Society in our Church, arose chiefly from the nature of its organization. It aided Congregationalists, Presbyterians, Lutherans, &c., but exercised no ecclesiastical control over its candidates. This enlarged and liberal policy was often held up in certain quarters, by way of contrast with the rigid and sectarian course pursued by the Board of Education, which required its beneficiaries to subscribe a pledge containing their assent to the Confession of Faith, and their purpose to become preachers of the gospel in the Presbyterian Church. The tendency of this comparison, in its influence upon the Presbyterian beneficiaries of the American Education Society, was to diminish their attachment to their own church; to make them feel that its doctrinal standards, according to their obvious and commonly received sense, were too rigid, unfriendly to revivals, and to the spirit of the age; and that these formularies must be understood in a lax sense, in order to enable those who adopt them to preach the gospel with sincerity, earnestness, and success.

The Home Missionary Society exerted an unfriendy influence among us in several ways. The policy of that Society, and perhaps its Constitution also, were antagonistic to strict Presbyterianism. It was at first the rival, and then the opponent of our own Board of Missions. What the latter was authorized and required to do, in order to check the progress of error, by refusing to commission unsound men, the former either could not constitutionally do, or did not attempt. Many of those sent out by this Society to labour in our churches, were more or less favourable to the "New Theology." Circumstances appeared also to indicate that in some instances their location was selected for them with reference to their "liberal" views concerning doctrine and polity. It was spoken of at the time, as being no uncommon event, for the majority in small Presbyteries to become, in a few months, the minority, by the accession of three or four missionaries of that Society. And in most cases, as members of our judicatories, whether in the majority or minority, they were found, on questions of doctrinal controversy, to argue and vote against the Old-school, and in favour of the New. From these particulars, it is easy to see what a powerful influence that Society was exerting over the several judicatories of the Presbyterian Church; and how difficult it was, under these circumstances, to obtain a verdict against the errors and irregularities which existed within our bounds. After a struggle of several years, the crisis at length arrived, and the General Assembly of 1837 adopted those decisive measures, which were condemned by one party as unconstitutional and oppressive, but regarded by the other as being authorized by the Constitution of the Church, and demanded by the necessity of the case. To those acts we will now direct our attention.

CHAPTER XI.

THE ACTS OF THE GENERAL ASSEMBLY IN 1837 AND 1838.

As the Plan of Union agreed to in 1801 by the General Assembly and the General Association of Connecticut, was believed to be a prolific source of the errors which had for some years disturbed the peace of our Church, the first act of the Assembly, touching the subject of reform, was the abrogation of that Plan. This was done in the following terms: "But as the 'Plan of Union' adopted for the new settlements, in 1801, was originally an unconstitutional act on the part of that Assembly—these important standing rules having never been submitted to the Presbyteries—and as they were totally destitute of authority as proceeding from the General Association of Connecticut, which is invested with no power to legislate in such cases, and especially to enact laws to regulate churches not within her limits; and as much confusion and irregularity have arisen from this unnatural and unconstitutional system of union; therefore, it is resolved, that the Act of the Assembly of 1801, entitled a 'Plan of Union,' be, and the same is hereby abrogated."

As this resolution was the basis of others which succeeded, it is important to correct two or three mistakes which appear to be current in certain quarters with regard to the Plan of Union. One of these relates to its origin. It has been often asserted that the General Assembly *proposed* the plan. This is a mistake. It has probably arisen from the fact, that the only authority which has been relied upon for the history of the affair, is the Assembly's Digest, which unfortunately contains only a part of the record. The Minutes of the Assembly for 1800 and 1801, show that the plan was proposed by the General Association of Connecticut, and not by the General Assembly.

In the Minutes for 1800, is the following: "The Rev. Dr. Jonathan Edwards, the Rev. Asa Hillyer and Jonathan Freeman were appointed delegates from this Assembly to the General Association of Connecticut," &c. Not a word is said about instructing them to negotiate a plan of union. In the Minutes of 1801 we find their report as follows: "The delegates from the General Assembly to the General Association of Connecticut report, that they all attended according to appointment through the whole course of the session of the General Association. That besides the business peculiar to the churches of Connecticut, the *General Association appointed a committee to confer with a committee that may be appointed by the General Assembly, on measures which may promote union among the inhabitants of the new settlements and the missionaries to those settlements, as appears by the enclosed paper.*" Immediately after the committee had reported, the paper referred to above was read, the minute concerning which is as follows: "A communication was read from the General Association of the State of Connecticut, appointing a committee to confer with a committee of the Presbyterian Church, to consider the measures proper to be adopted by the General Association and the General Assembly, for establishing a uniform system of church government between the inhabitants of the new settlements who are attached to the Presbyterian form of government, and those who prefer the Congregational form. Ordered that the said communication lie on the table. Succeeding this, on the same page, is the following: "The Rev. Drs. Edwards, McKnight and Woodhull, the Rev. Mr. Blatchford and Hutton, were appointed a committee to consider and digest a plan of government for the churches in the new settlements, *agreeably to the proposal of the General Association of Connecticut*, and report the same as soon as convenient."

Again—it has been often affirmed, that during the whole period of thirty-six years, in which this plan was in operation [prior to 1837,] *no objection* was made to it; and consequently it is to be considered as having received during this long period the silent approbation of the whole church. But this is a mistake. First, it is not true, in the sense intended by those who revert to it, that the Plan had been in operation for so long a time—I mean in such a sense as to give to the fact that force which it is supposed to have in determining its validity. For ten or twelve years after it was formed, its influence upon the church was scarcely felt; and for as many more, the evils growing out of it had not developed themselves as they did after that time. The Plan was originally intended not as a medium through which Congregationalism would be perpetuated in the Presbyterian Church, but to afford opportunity for Congregationalists, (if after learning the character of our system they approved of it) to become Presbyterian. This remark applies to both parties in the arrangement. The *ministers* of Connecticut were favourable to the Presbyterian form of government; one feature of it was already in existence in their churches, and they were

willing (not to say desirous) to have their people, who should emigrate to other States, become Presbyterian. This idea, we think, is clearly implied in the account which has been published of the interview of the committee of the Assembly with a committee of the Association in 1826. "As to the union, they said, (the Connecticut committee) that it had not been gone into for their accommodation, but for ours; that they had agreed to it for two reasons: first, because it was a help to many New England people in the infant settlements towards obtaining gospel ordinances: and secondly, *because it assisted the Assembly in spreading Presbyterianism through that region.*" But instead of spreading Presbyterianism, it spread, in a large number of cases, Congregationalism under the Presbyterian name. Presbyteries were not only formed of Congregational materials, but with an express stipulation placed at the beginning of their Records, that they might always remain so, and yet continue in the Presbyterian Church.*
And then, by such a construction of the Plan of Union as was never intended by the original framers, they claimed the right of sending commissioners, who were not ruling elders, to the General Assembly. This is the point of time at which the Plan ought to be dated, if it is designed to have any bearing on the constitutional question; because at this time, and not before,

---

* See a pamphlet entitled "Facts and Observations," &c. published by the author in 1837. Some of the matter contained in it is now transferred to these pages.

were its effects upon our church order fully manifest; and this would be not thirty-six years, but less than twenty.

We are now prepared to observe, secondly, that as soon as these effects of the Plan of Union were perceived, objections began to be made to it, and they were repeated at different times, and in one form or another, until its abrogation. In 1826, a commissioner from the Rochester Presbytery was received by the Assembly, who was not a ruling elder; but a protest was immediately entered against it, signed by forty-two members. In 1831, a committee-man was received by the Assembly as a commissioner from the Grand River Presbytery, against which sixty-seven members entered their protest. A part of this protest is as follows: "The articles of agreement alluded to in the beginning of this paper," (referring to the Plan of Union of 1801,) "are supposed to give this individual, and all others similarly situated, a seat in this Assembly. That agreement is altogether anomalous to our form of government, and, so far as it does extend, is in derogation of it." . . . . "Those articles can never cover this case, because they expressly stipulate the church session and Presbytery, as the church courts to which these 'committee-men' may have access, in the character of ruling elders, and mention no others." . . . . "If, however, they are so construed as to place members here who are, by our constitution, forbidden to be here, or as in any degree to affect the principles of the organization of this house, as clearly defined in our books, then it is manifest that the articles must be considered utterly *null* and *void.*"

Though the Assembly received the commissioner above referred to, they adopted a resolution that "the appointment, by some Presbyteries, as has occurred in a few cases, of members of standing committees to be members of the General Assembly, is inexpedient, and of questionable constitutionality, and therefore ought not, in future, to be made." The next year, that same Presbytery delegated two committee-men as commissioners to the Assembly; but their commissions, after having been placed in the hands of a committee, were withdrawn. At the same meeting, there was a commissioner from a Presbytery in Western New York, who was neither an elder nor a committee-man; but being commissioned as an elder, and no one present being acquainted with the circumstance, or disposed to make it known, he was received as a member. The year following a committee-man appeared from the Presbytery of Oswego, and would have been received, (as his commission did not specify his true character,) had not a member who had incidentally become acquainted with the fact, made it known to the house, when leave was given him to withdraw his commission. These facts show with what tenacity those Presbyteries which were formed in pursuance of the Plan of Union, persisted in the practice of sending up commissioners, even after the Assembly had adopted a resolution against it; and the course which the Assembly pursued in regard to them, was an expression of disapprobation against *their interpretation* of the Plan, if not against the Plan itself. In 1835, the Assembly resolved that no more churches should be organized on the Plan of Union, and in 1837 the plan was abrogated. Thus for eleven years previous to this last act, there was evidently a growing dissatisfaction with the manner in which the Plan of Union was found to operate; its constitutionality was more than once called in question, and intimations were given, in no doubtful language, that the Assembly ought either to " amend or annul" it.

With regard to the measure itself—it has been objected that the Assembly were bound, before passing such an act, to ask the consent of the other contracting party—meaning thereby either the General Association of Connecticut, or the churches formed on the Plan of Union. Were they bound to ask the consent of the Association? For an answer to this question, we refer the reader to the opinion of George Wood, Esq., given in 1837, at the request of some of our New-school brethren. " I do not think that this Plan of Union formed, or was the result of a compact between the General Assembly and the Association of Connecticut, so as to render it obligatory upon the General Assembly to carry into effect the measure, or to continue its operation any longer than they should deem proper." . . . . . . " It may be questioned whether the assent of the Association to the adoption by the Assembly of this Plan was necessary. The Congregationalists to be affected by this Plan were out of the jurisdiction of that Association, and beyond their control; but they no doubt felt themselves under a moral influence, which rendered it a matter of delicacy and expediency on the part of the General Assembly to obtain the assent of that Association. But supposing the assent of the Association to have been indispensable when it was given, they had nothing further to do with the Plan. *It then became the measure of the General Assembly alone, to be dropped, or acted upon, or modified as they should deem advisable."* If this opinion be correct, then the churches alone, if any body, were the party to be consulted. On this point we need only observe, that if there is obligation on either side to ask the consent of the other before the connection might be dissolved, this obligation must be equally binding upon both. But did the churches ever feel any obligation of this kind? Did they not always consider it as optional with them, either to continue their connection with the Presbyterian Church, to become independent, or join an Association, without asking the consent of the General Assembly? As a matter of courtesy, they usually notified the Presbytery to which they belonged, that they were about to change their ecclesiastical connection; but not from a belief of the existence of any contract with the Presbytery, which obliged them to do so; and it frequently happened that the Presbyteries had no knowledge of their intention, until after the formation of their new alliances. If, therefore, the churches formed on the Plan of Union did not understand the Plan as involving any obligation upon themselves of the kind supposed, it would be unreasonable in them to maintain that any such obligation rested on the Assembly, or to expect that an overture should have been made to them by the Assembly, asking their consent for a dissolution of the union.

FURTHER PROCEEDINGS OF THE ASSEMBLY.

The bond which connected the three Synods of Western New York and the Synod of the Western Reserve with the General Assembly being now sundered, it was a grave question for the Assembly to consider, whether they should proceed to declare this fact, and thence regard and treat those Synods as being separated from the Presbyterian Church, and of course no longer amenable to the Assembly; or whether the separation of the Congregational from the Presbyterian materials, should be effected through the action of Presbyteries and churches. There were in those Presbyteries ministers and churches, or at least parts of churches, thoroughly Presbyterian, whose rights and privileges were in some way to be provided for; but the number of Congregationalists was so large as to render it very difficult, if not impracticable, to carry out the views of the Assembly through the action of Presbyteries or churches. On the other hand, there were in some Synods not owing their existence to the Plan of Union, a few Congretional churches, whose future relations were to be determined by some method of proceeding to be adopted by the Assembly; and would it not be best to pursue a uniform course with regard to all? These were questions which demanded serious deliberation. Accordingly no further action was taken on this subject for a day or two; and the Assembly resolved to introduce judicial process against "such inferior judicatories as should appear to be charged by common fame with the toleration of gross errors in doctrine and disorders in practice." This resolution was carried by a majority of 6 only—122 voting in the negative and 102 entering their protest against it! What hope was there that citations issued under such circumstances, would be of any avail? This vote, and the previous one abrogating the Plan of Union, (on which 110 voted in the negative,) showed also how ineffectual would be the attempt to reach the evils complained of, by directing the Presbyteries or churches to take action based on the abrogation of that Plan. A determination was manifested by the commissioners from those Synods, and by the New-school party in general, to adhere to the Plan, and to preserve the integrity of the churches which had been formed under it.

Judicial proceedings appearing to be impracticable, a proposition was next made, on the part of the Old-school, for a voluntary separation of the two parties in the church, and a committee of ten was appointed, five on each side, to confer together and report to the Assembly a plan for an amicable division. This committee agreed upon "the propriety of a voluntary separation," "the corporate funds, the names to be held by each denomination, the records of the church, and its boards and institutions." But they differed "as to the propriety of entering at once by the Assembly upon the division;" "as to the power of the Assembly to take effectual initiative steps, as proposed by the majority"—*i. e.* by the Old-school members; the New wishing to refer the question to the Presbyteries; and "as to the breaking up of the succession of that General Assembly, so that neither of the new Assemblies proposed be considered *that* proper body continued;" in regard to which the Old-school portion of the committee "could not consent to any thing that should even imply the final dissolution of the Presbyterian Church as now organized in this country;" though they "were perfectly disposed to do all that the utmost liberality could demand, and to use in all cases such expressions. as should be wholly unexceptionable." The committee failing to agree, each portion presented to the Assembly a separate report, and the subject was dropped.

The Assembly then proceeded to carry into effect the resolution before adopted, abrogating the Plan of Union. They declared first, the Synod of the Western Reserve to be "no longer a part of the Presbyterian Church in the United States of America;" and afterwards adopted a similar resolution with regard to the Synods of Utica, Geneva, and Genessee. Though the Assembly assigned as their reason for this course, and their "urgency for the immediate decision of it," the "gross disorders which were ascertained to have prevailed in those Synods;" they nevertheless affirmed as to their present action, that they had "no intention, by these resolutions," . . . . "to affect in any way the ministerial standing of any members of either of said Synods; nor to disturb the pastoral relations of any church; nor to interfere with the duties or relations of private Christians in their respective congregations; but only to declare and determine according to the truth and necessity of the case, and by virtue of the full authority existing in [the Assembly] for that purpose, the relation of all said Synods and all their constituent parts to that body, and to the Presbyterian Church in the United States." The Assembly also provided that any ministers and churches in those Synods that were strictly Presbyterian in doctrine and order, might be exempted from the operation of these resolutions, by applying to the Presbyteries in our connection most convenient to them; and that Presbyteries of this character might be exempted, by making a statement of their case to the next General Assembly.

The Assembly likewise dissolved the Third Presbytery of Philadelphia, and "recommended" that the American Home Missionary Society and the American Education Society "should cease to operate within any of our churches." These measures require no special vindication at present—as the authority of the Assembly to adopt them was not denied by our New-school brethren; though for other reasons they were opposed to their adoption. The motives which influenced the Assembly to their action with regard to those Societies, have been alluded to already in the preceding chapter, and also in the Preface to the first edition, published in 1838.

With regard to the propriety of those acts, styled opprobriously, in New-school prints, the "exscinding" acts, the discussion of two questions will embrace all that is necessary to a correct decision of the case. The first is, Was it a legitimate and constitutional mode of proceeding, for the Assembly to act upon Synods as such? And the second, Had those four Synods any such connection with the Plan of Union, as to be virtually separated from the Assembly and the Presbyterian Church, by its abrogation? As to the first—According to our form of government, the higher judicatories possess the power of review and control over the lower; and in carrying out this principle, the ordinary mode of action is for the next higher to take cognizance of that which is immediately below it. The Presbytery acts on the church, by directing the session; and the Synod on both the session and church, by an order directed to the Presbytery. In like manner, the General Assembly usually acts on the lower judicatories through the Synods. Though that body is not bound invariably to this course, it will not be denied by any acquainted with our Constitution, that this is not only a legitimate one, but that it ought not to be departed from, except for special reasons. Suppose, in the case under consideration, the Assembly had attempted to act upon the Presbyteries, or (as some maintained they ought to have done) directly upon the churches. In the former case it might have been said, they had assumed the prerogatives of the Synod, and in the latter, that they had taken into their hands a work which belonged exclusively to the Presbyteries. Those who opposed the measures of the Assembly, would have objected with as much earnestness, we have reason to believe, to the other course. Many of them did virtually object to it soon after in their Presbyteries, by the adoption of resolutions "assuring the churches under their care, that the Plan of Union, so far as they were concerned, was still in force, and its stipulations would be preserved by them inviolate."

It was urged against the application of the vote to *Synods*, that those bodies, as such, *could* not have been formed on the Plan of Union, but were regularly constituted according to the directions of the Book; and therefore they could not be affected by the abrogation of the Plan. As to the *manner* in which Synods are brought into existence, we admit that all of them, except the first, must necessarily be organized alike, viz: by the division of other Synods— and again, that they all must necessarily be alike, in being composed of at least three Presbyteries. But suppose one or two of the three Presbyteries of which a particular Synod is composed, though they bear the name of Presbyteries, are in reality Congregational Associations; would the Synod in this case be regularly constituted? Or suppose the Presbyteries generally of which it is composed, though consisting in part of Presbyterian churches, have in them so large a number of Congregationalists, as to give to the Presbyteries a Congregational character; would a Synod composed of such Presbyteries be a regular Synod according to our Constitution? Must it not, on the contrary, be styled, speaking in strict propriety, a *Congregational Synod*, however agreeable to the Constitution may have been the *mere form* of its erection? On the same principle, though churches alone, in the first instance, could be organized on the Plan of Union, yet as churches, in connection with their pastors, compose Presbyteries, and Presbyteries compose Synods; if such a number of the churches are formed on this Plan as to control the action and policy of the Presbyteries and Synods, the latter, for aught we can perceive to the contrary, must also be regarded as organized on the Plan of Union.

Again:—it is objected that this mode of applying the act operated *unjustly;* as many of the churches in those Synods were strictly Presbyterian. If this objection be valid, it would effectually have closed the door against any action whatever; except by dissolving the churches formed on the Plan of Union, and directing them to organize anew—at least, all such churches as are partly composed of Presbyterian members. There would be the same reason to complain of the *injustice* of an act, which disowns a Presbyterian *member*, as of one that disowns a church. It is true that the mode of remedying an evil by acting upon communities, often if not always subjects individuals among them to temporary inconvenience, who, if they were not thus connected, could not justly be brought into such circumstances. But, if the measure is necessary for the public good, and provision is made by which (if they avail themselves of it) they will not in the end be affected injuriously, they ought not to complain—especially if the evil to be remedied could not be reached in any other way.

In order to ascertain whether those acts were *just*, it is important to understand their true nature. Were they acts of *excommunication* as some affirm? or did they leave the disowned Synods in this respect, just as they stood before? The effect of excommunication is to suspend ministers from their clerical functions, and church members from Christian communion. Was this done, or designed to be done by the General Assembly? If their disclaimer at the time of adopting those resolutions be not deemed sufficient, the uniform conduct of the Old-school towards the New in their official and Christian intercourse with them, has been from that time to the present, a standing rebuke to those who attempt to excite popular indignation against the Assembly, on the ground that those Synods have been "exscinded," "cut off," "expelled," without citation or trial. Those acts, it is true, implied some censure. But its severity was greatly softened, and with regard to the sound portion of them, entirely removed by the form in which it was administered. There was no citation or trial, because all judicial proceedings were dropped; and the Assembly simply said to them, "We will not disturb your ecclesiastical relations as they exist among yourselves; but we cannot consent to have the Presbyterian Church revolutionized and remodelled through your instrumentality; especially, as you came into it at first only by courtesy and compromise; and we therefore regard it as right and proper to inform you, that from this time forward, you shall not be represented in our body." Is not this a fair statement of what the Assembly did? If so, (and we believe it cannot be successfully controverted,) we cannot perceive any substantial reason for the charge of injustice—especially as the individuals and churches who (as is alleged) ought to have been excepted, were expressly informed that the door was left open for them to reunite with the Assembly, if they should think this to be more for their edification and for the glory of God, than to remain connected with those Synods. Chief Justice Gibson, in giving the opinion of the Court in bank in 1839, observed as follows: "The apparent injustice of the measure arises from the contemplation of it as a judicial sentence, pronounced against parties who were neither cited nor heard, which it evidently was not. Even as a legislative act, it may have been a hard one, though certainly constitutional, and strictly just."

If then the Assembly acted constitutionally and justly in applying those resolutions to Synods taken as a body, the only question which remains to be settled is, Had those four Synods such a connection with the Plan of Union, that their separation from the General Assembly and the Presbyterian Church was a legitimate consequence of its abrogation? With regard to the Synod of the Western Reserve, there is no ground for doubt. A member of that Synod, the Rev. J. Seward, in an article communicated to the *Ohio Observer*, in 1837, wrote as follows: "The Presbytery of Grand River, agreeably to the order of the Synod of Pittsburgh, was organized in the autumn of 1814, and as it covered ground on which a union had been established between Presbyterians and Congregationalists, according to the regulations adopted by the General Assembly of the Presbyterian Church, it was deemed necessary that this Presbytery should be so organized as to consolidate and perpetuate this union, and thus carry out the recommendations and injunctions of the General Assembly. To accomplish this object, a number of articles, adapted to the peculiar situation of the churches in this region, was adopted by this Presbytery, and afterwards by the Presbyteries of Portage and Huron, as they were respectively organized. The design of these articles was to secure to all connected with these Presbyteries the rights and privileges pledged in the regulations adopted by the General Assembly and the General Association in 1801." . . . . "At a meeting of the General Assembly in 1825, a petition was presented for a division of the Synod of Pittsburgh, and the erection of a new Synod, to be composed of the three Presbyteries above named, and to be known by the name of the Synod of the Western Reserve. This request was granted." . . . . . . From this statement it will be perceived that the three Presbyteries of which this Synod was composed, were formed explicitly on the Plan of Union. Had it not been for that Plan, neither they nor the Synod could have been organized.

The oldest of the three Synods in Western New York is Geneva; which was constituted in 1812, by a division of the Synod of Albany, and consisted at that time of three Presbyteries, viz: Geneva, Cayuga, and Onondaga. The Geneva Presbytery was formed from the Presbytery of Oneida in 1805; at which time the latter Presbytery reported twenty churches, about one-half of which appear to have been Congregational; and as that part of its territory which was set off to form the Geneva Presbytery, was particularly intended for the operation of the Plan of Union, it is reasonable to infer that a large proportion of the churches belonging to the new Presbytery were Congregational. But my information with regard to it, is not so definite as concerning the other two Presbyteries. In 1808, the Synod of Albany, by permission of the General Assembly, received the Middle Association of the Western District, as a constituent part of that Synod. In 1809, it reported to the Synod twenty-one congregations; and in the Minutes of the General Assembly for that year and the year following, the Association is named in the statistical account. In 1810, the Presbytery of Geneva and the "Middle Association" made a joint request to Synod to be organized into three Presbyteries, which was accordingly done. By this arrangement, that part of Geneva Presbytery which lay east of Cayuga lake, was detached from it (containing, however, but a single church) and in connection with the churches belonging to the Association, two Presbyteries were formed, viz: Cayuga and Onondaga; the former having fifteen and the latter thirteen churches. Eight years afterwards (1819) these two Presbyteries were doubled by accessions from the Onondaga Association, which was dissolved and its ministers and churches received into these Presbyteries on the Plan of Union.

Several of the Presbyteries which were subsequently added to the Synod had a similar origin. One of them (Cortland) can be traced to the Middle Association. Two others, viz: Chenango and Delaware, derived their materials from the Union Association; which was dissolved, or rather "broken up," by the action of its ministers; who without the consent or knowledge of their churches, joined the Otsego Presbytery; immediately after which, the Presbytery applied to the General Assembly, to form them into a new Presbytery, to be called Chenango; which request being granted, the Presbytery was formed in 1826, consisting of ministers only. A plan of union was adopted by the new Presbytery on the basis of the action of the General Assembly in 1808, soon after which most of their churches united with the Presbytery. The Delaware Presbytery was formed from a part of Chenango, and of course had the same origin.

From these facts, it appears that the Synod of Geneva not only grew out of the Plan of Union, but that when it was organized, it had not sufficient materials to form a *Constitutional* Synod. Two of its three original Presbyteries, were the twin daughters of the Middle Association, whose name had been dropped, but the organization of its churches continued to be substantially the same as before. Nor did the growth of the Synod for fifteen years afterwards materially change its character in this respect. Two other Congregational associations were dissolved during this period, and without any change in their form of government as churches, or with very slight ones it may be in some cases, were received into the different Presbyteries of this Synod. The reader must recollect that we do not mention these things as a crime, but only to show what is the constitutional relation of this Synod to the Presbyterian Church.

The Synod of Genessee was constituted in 1821, by a division of the Synod of Geneva, and consisted of four Presbyteries, viz: Niagara, Ontario, Genessee, and Rochester. I name them in the order of their organization. The first two were formed in 1817, from the Presbytery of Geneva; and the last two in 1819, from the Presbytery of Ontario. The Genessee Presbytery, at the time or soon after it was formed, adopted a paper containing an exposition of the Plan of Union, and transcribed it in their Presbyterial Records, for the information of the churches under their care. Whether any of the other Presbyteries adopted a similar course on this subject, I am not informed. But from the testimony of personal friends and acquaintances, who then resided in the bounds of this Synod, I feel no hesitation in saying, that the prevailing impression in all the Presbyteries was, that they grew up under the Plan of Union;

and that previously to 1837, the churches in general were so much attached to this Plan, viewed as a modification of Presbyterian government, that rather than give it up, they would have seceded from the Presbyterian Church, and have become wholly Congregational.

The Synod of Utica was constituted in 1829, by a division of the Synod of Albany, and consisted of five Presbyteries, viz: Oneida, Watertown, Otsego, St. Lawrence, and Oswego. Though this Synod is the youngest of the three in Western New York, one of its Presbyteries, viz: Oneida, is the oldest of all. It was formed from a part of the Presbytery of Albany in 1802, one year after the date of the Plan of Union. It consisted at that time of six ministers. No churches are named; but from an examination of the statistical reports of the Presbytery of Albany up to this time, it will appear that there were five or six churches embraced in the territory assigned to the new Presbytery. In 1803 it had seventeen, and in 1805, twenty churches, about one-half of which were Congregational. The next year it reported but eight, the others having been detached to form the Presbytery of Geneva. From this time there was a gradual increase till 1816, when there was an accession of twelve ministers and nine churches. All the ministers except one were from Congregational Associations; and all the churches, it is believed, were Congregational. This large accession was owing to the dissolution of the Oneida Association, which has been represented as an interesting and flourishing body; but as the Plan of Union opened a door for their admission into the Presbyterian Church, and as the ministers were desirous of forming such a connection, the people were persuaded to yield. The Association was accordingly dissolved, and most of its ministers and churches joined the Presbytery.

The Presbytery of Watertown (called at first St. Lawrence) was constituted from the Oneida Presbytery in 1816, consisting of five ministers and two churches. In 1819, the number of churches reported to the General Assembly was eleven, seven of which were Congregational. Their history in this respect, from that time onward, I am unable to give. But the Congregational character of the Presbytery taken as a body, may be inferred from a fact related to me in 1834 or 1835, by a clerical brother who had resided ten or twelve months in that section of the State; viz: that a number of ministers in that Presbytery belonged to a Congregational Association, and were acting members both of the Presbytery and Association at the same time; that in one case a candidate, who was refused license by the Presbytery, applied immediately afterwards to a part of the same men, who, laying aside their Presbyterial character, and acting in the capacity of Congregational ministers, made out and subscribed his licensure. The Otsego and Oswego Presbyteries were also constituted from the Presbytery of Oneida; the former in 1819, and and the latter in 1822. As the materials for these Presbyteries were derived mainly from the Oneida Association, an account of which has just been given, their connection with the Plan of Union is sufficiently manifest, without any particular statement concerning their churches. In 1837, one-half of those in Otsego Presbytery were Congregational, and in the Oswego Presbytery two-thirds.

The St. Lawrence Presbytery (called at first Ogdensburg) was constituted in 1821, by a division of the Presbytery of Champlain. The latter Presbytery, previous to this time, extended over the whole territory of Northern New York, and was in a great degree missionary ground. Many of the churches in that region were organized by an excellent and laborious Congregational missionary,* whom I have heard relate many thrilling incidents concerning his labours, his discouragements, and his success. I heard him also, at the same time, express his partiality for the Congregational mode of government; and listened to one of his sermons, which he read to several persons present, and which had been delivered by him on a former occasion, a part of which was designed to show, by way of contrast, the superior excellence of Congregationalism. Some of the churches which he formed were, perhaps, Presbyterian; but the major part were undoubtedly Congregational; and as those churches composed afterwards (at least in part) the St. Lawrence Presbytery, it is highly probable that it had for its basis the Plan of Union.

We have thus noticed each of the Presbyteries belonging to this Synod, and the result is, that all of

* He belonged to the Northern Associated Presbytery.

them except one were Congregational in their origin, and continued to be more or less so in their elements, form and spirit, after they were constituted as Presbyteries. And the same we have found to be true concerning the other two Synods. If this statement needs corroborating by other proof, I can adduce the testimony of one of the oldest ministers in Western New York, the Rev. Mr. Hotchkin, author of a History of the Churches there, and a member of the Auburn Convention in 1837. In a speech made by him on that occasion, he said that "the churches in the three Synods of Western New York" (with the exception of two or three which were formed on the plan of 1801) came in on the plan of 1808, when the Northern Associated Presbytery, and the Middle Association of the Western District, were received by the Synod of Albany.* In 1809, the delegates from the Middle Association were received in the General Assembly, and their names, together with the name of the Association, appear on the minutes of the Assembly of that year. But the Association soon lost its name, and in con-

* The action of that Synod, so far as it related to the Northern Associated Presbytery, did not go into effect for many years. The older ministers belonging to this body were opposed to the change; and out of regard to their feelings, the Presbytery was not dissolved until they had either died or consented to join some other Congregational Association; at which time, (not earlier than 1815 or 1816,) the one or two ministers that remained, united with the Presbytery of Albany. Not long afterwards, eight or ten of the churches joined the same Presbytery—about half of them having previously changed their organization, by appointing ruling elders.

nection with the Presbytery of Geneva, which was organized several years, three Presbyteries were formed out of it, viz: Geneva, Cayuga, and Onondaga. The Onondaga Association was afterwards dissolved, by the advice of the Rev. Mr. Chapman, and received by the Synod of Geneva on the same plan." Speaking of these churches having for several years waived their right (as he regarded it) to be represented in the General Assembly, in order to avoid difficulty, he said that he had great influence in bringing about the change; and that if he had not exerted his influence in the case, instead of there being three Synods, there would probably have been now (1837) but one Presbytery."

The connection of those four Synods with the Presbyterian Church, on the basis of the Plan of Union, having been (as we think) sufficiently established, it follows, that the action of the General Assembly concerning them was authorized, if not required, by the operation of the previous resolution adopted by the Assembly abrogating that Plan. In this conclusion I am sustained by the Court in bank for the State of Pennsylvania, whose opinion was delivered by Chief Justice Gibson, in 1839. His language is as follows: "Surely this [Plan of Union] was not intended to outlast the inability of the respective sects to provide separately for themselves, or to perpetuate the innovations on Presbyterian government which it was calculated to produce. It was obviously a missionary arrangement from the first; and they who built up Presbyteries and Synods on the basis of it, had no reason to expect that their structures would survive it, or that Congregationalists might, by force of it, gain a foothold in the Presbyterian Church, despite of Presbyterian discipline. They embraced it with all its defeasible properties plainly put before them; and the power which constituted it might fairly repeal it, and dissolve the bodies that had grown out of it, whenever the good of the church should seem to require it."

As we have quoted a part of the opinion of the Court in this case, it may not be amiss to make a remark or two concerning its final decision. The trial before the Court of Nisi Prius resulted in favour of the New-school party; in view of which the closing words of the opinion delivered by the Court in bank were—" Rule for a new trial made absolute." This has been represented in New-school publications as deciding nothing in favour of the Old-school except to grant them an opportunity for another hearing; whereas it was a virtual decision of the whole case in their favour. Every important principle involved in it was fully discussed, and the concluding sentences, preceding the grant for a new trial, were as follows: "Other corroborative views have been suggested; but it is difficult to compress a decision of the leading points in this case into the old fashioned limits of a judicial opinion. The preceding observations, however, are deemed enough to show the grounds on which we hold that the Assembly which met in the First Presbyterian Church (*i. e.* the New-school Assembly) was not the legitimate successor of the Assembly of 1837, and that the defendants (the Old-school) are not guilty of the usurpation with which they are charged." Were these words intended to decide nothing touching the merits of the case? The New-school, and not the Old, were the plaintiffs; and hence the former, and not the latter, were the party to renew the prosecution, if a new trial was ever to be had. Why did they not recommence the suit? For this obvious reason, that there was no hope of success. Every point on which the decision of the case depended, was ruled in favour of the Old-school Assembly.

In 1838 the commissioners appointed by the Presbyteries belonging to the four Synods above named, and those from other Presbyteries who chose to act with them, formed a separate General Assembly, and appealed to the civil court to sustain them in their new position. The result of the suit we have just noticed. There being now two bodies, the Old-school Assembly, in order to perfect those measures of reform which had been commenced the preceding year, and to make special provision for the future, adopted a paper containing three acts; which provided for the reception of all such ministers and church members as were thrown by circumstances with the Presbyteries represented in the new Assembly, but who might desire to remain with the Old-school body; and directed them particularly what course to pursue in order to be recognized by the Assembly. These acts were designed to operate, on the one hand, as a check to the continuance in our communion of any who might entertain loose doctrinal views; and on the other, as an expression of cordial welcome to the admission of all who adopted the Confession of Faith according to its obvious sense. Some words and phrases which they contained, were unfortunately ambiguous; on which account objections were made to them by various persons, who understood them as requiring those who adhered to the Old-school Assembly to express their *approbation* of the acts of the Assembly in 1837 and 1838. Objections were also made to them on other grounds. An explanatory resolution was accordingly adopted in 1843, declaring that "in requiring an adherence to our church on the basis of the Assembly of 1837 and 1838, they (the Assembly) did not create nor introduce any new basis of Presbyterianism, but required an adherence to the true and only basis of our organization and communion, viz: the doctrinal standards and constitution of our church, as founded on the word of God, a deplorable departure from which had been suffered through the operation of the Plan of Union." And further, "that it was not then, and is not now, required of those who would adhere to us as a branch of the church of Christ, that, as a term of membership in this church, they should approve the acts of the Assembly of 1837 and 1838; but simply that they should recognize the church as then and subsequently constituted as the Presbyterian Church in the United States of America, and acknowledge their subjection to its judicatories." This explanation was intended partly to disabuse the minds of those who desired to unite with us, but could not assent to the required conditions, according to their understanding of the acts of the Assembly of

1838, and partly to vindicate the Assembly from the charge which had been opprobriously made against them, of establishing a "new basis" wholly unknown to the constitution. Our New-school brethren maintained that there could not be a constitutional General Assembly without admitting the commissioners from the four Synods of Western New York and the Western Reserve. The acts of the Assembly of 1838, assuming that what had been done the preceding year on this subject was "constitutional and just," required of those who would unite with us, an adherence to the Assembly as then constituted, and a recognition of it as the true General Assembly. They could not have required less than this without receding from the ground which they had taken, re-enacting the Plan of Union, and restoring those Synods to their former connection with the Presbyterian Church.

The question, which of the two Assemblies of 1838 was the true General Assembly, the legitimate and legal successor of the Assembly of 1837 may be easily determined. Our New-school brethren admit that the acts of the Assembly of 1837 excluding the four Synods, did not destroy that body or render their subsequent acts during the same sessions invalid. They found their claim to the succession on the manner of constituting the Assembly of 1838. The standing committee of commissions, agreeably to the instructions of the preceding Assembly, refused at the opening of the sessions of 1838, to enrol the names of the commissioners from the Presbyteries belonging to these four Synods, and the moderator declared it out of order to put to the house a motion which was offered, touching this subject, until the Assembly should be organized by the election of a new moderator; whereupon the New-school commissioners, by the advice, as they said, of "counsel learned in the law," proceeded immediately to appoint a new moderator and clerks, and then adjourned to meet in another house, leaving the Old-school portion in the quiet occupancy of their seats. By this manœuvre they claim to have deposed the moderator and to have elected another in his place; and then after having in like manner elected new clerks, to have carried with them as they left the house the true and legal succession. The silence of the Old-school commissioners while these hasty and disorderly proceedings were going on, is construed by them as having been a legal acquiescence in this extraordinary movement. A few considerations will place this matter in its true light.

1. If the acts of the Assembly of 1837 disowning the four Synods were "constitutional and strictly just," as was affirmed by the Court in bank for the State of Pennsylvania, then the exclusion of the commissioners from those Synods in 1838, was constitutional and just, because this was nothing more than adhering to what had been done the preceding year.

2. The refusal of the clerks to enrol the names of those commissioners, whether right or wrong, did not prevent the Assembly of 1838 from being validly constituted, our New-school brethren themselves being judges. The tender of those commissions to the

house through the moderator, by one of their number, and his motion to have their names enrolled, assumed that there was a regular moderator in the chair, and a judicatory thus far validly constituted; for otherwise they were not competent to receive and act upon his motion.

3. If, then, the legal existence of the body was destroyed at all, this was done by the suicidal act of the moderator who refused to put the motion, on the ground that it was out of order. On this point let it be remembered, that though at the time these commissions were offered, he had just called for additional commissions, if there were any in the house which had not been presented to the clerks; this call applied exclusively to those concerning whose right to seats there was no doubt, and not to commissions refused by the clerks. Contested rights could not properly be debated and settled at that time, as the next business in order was to elect a new moderator; after which, commissions of this description might either be considered by the Assembly, or referred to a special committee on elections to examine and report thereon. The moderator was therefore not at fault in this particular. But on the supposition that it was his duty to put the motion (which we do not admit) his refusal to do so did not depose him from office. This could be done, (even though it should be conceded that he deserved deposition) in no other way than by a distinct motion to this effect, and a vote of the house upon such motion; which it is not pretended was done or attempted.

4. It follows therefore, that the proceedings of the New-school commissioners, which were based on the assumption that the moderator's chair was virtually vacated by his own act, had no foundation in truth; and hence those proceedings did not possess either ecclesiastical or legal validity to effect the end which their members who participated in them had in view. The body which they thought proper to leave, contained at the time, and after the New-school members left the house, all the regularly constituted officers of the Assembly, and a majority of all the commissioners in attendance. The New-school members organized *a* General Assembly; but it was another and a different body from *the* General Assembly of 1837—38; the constitutional links of connection between the two not being possessed by them; while in the organization of the Old-school Assembly were found all the requisite elements of a true and legal succession.

The following extract from the opinion of the Court in bank already referred to, fully sustains us in these views. "It appears, therefore, (*i. e.* it follows from the preceding argument) that the commissioners from the exscinded Synods, were not entitled to seats in the Assembly, and that their names were properly excluded from the roll. The inquiry might be rested here; for if there was no colour of right in them, there was no colour of right in the adversary proceedings which were founded on their exclusion. But even if their title were clear, the refusal of an appeal from the decision of the moderator, would be no ground for the degradation of the officer at the call of a minority; nor could it impose on the majority an obligation to vote on a question put unofficially, and out of the usual course. To all questions put by the established organ, it is the duty of every member to respond, or be counted with the greater number, because he is supposed to have assented beforehand to the result of the process pre-established to ascertain the general will; but the rule of implied assent is certainly inapplicable to a measure which, when justifiable even by extreme necessity, is essentially revolutionary, and based on no pre-established process of ascertainment whatever.

"To apply it to an extreme case of inorganic action, as was done here, might work the degradation of any presiding officer in our legislative halls, by the motion and actual vote of a single member, sustained by the constructive votes of all the rest; and though such an enterprise may never be attempted, it shows the danger of resorting to a conventional rule, when the body is to be resolved into its original elements, and the rules and conventions to be superseded, by the very motion. For this reason, the choice of a moderator to supplant the officer in the chair, even if he were removable at the pleasure of the commissioners, would seem to have been unconstitutional.

"But he was not removable by them, because he had not derived his office from them; nor was he answerable to them for the use of his power. He was not *their* moderator. He was the mechanical instrument of their organization; and till that was accomplished, they were subject to his rule—not he to theirs. They were chosen by the authority of his mandate, and with the power of self-organization, only in the event of his absence at the opening of the session. Corporally present, but refusing to perform his functions, he might be deemed constructively absent, for constitutional purposes, insomuch that the commissioners might proceed to the choice of a substitute without him; but not if he had entered on the performance of his task; and the reason is that the decision of such questions as were prematurely pressed here, is proper for the decision of the body when prepared for organic action, which it cannot be before it is fully constituted, and under the presidency of its own moderator; the moderator of the preceding session being *functus officio*. . . . . . It seems, then, that an appeal from the decision of the moderator did not lie; and that he incurred no penalty by the disallowance of it. The title of the exscinded commissioners could be determined only by the action of the house, which could not be had before its organization was complete; and, in the mean time, he was bound, as the executive instrument of the preceding Assembly, to put its ordinance into execution; for to the actual Assembly, and not to the moderator of the preceding one, it belonged to repeal it."

CHAPTER XII.

PRESENT CHARACTER AND CONDITION OF THE OLD AND NEW-SCHOOL BODIES.

As nearly fifteen years have transpired since the division of the Presbyterian Church into two bodies, there has been sufficient opportunity for judging whether those causes which contributed to produce the separation were real or imaginary; temporary or permanent. It has never been denied that a subordinate cause of the division was the difference in the views of the two parties concerning voluntary societies and ecclesiastical boards; though this of itself could not have resulted in the formation of two distinct churches. No better evidence of this could be required than the fact, that since that time our New-school brethren have so nearly approximated to the views of the Old-school church on this subject, that if this were all, or even the chief cause of our separation, the union of the two divisions could at present be very easily effected. But, though in this respect we now occupy nearly the same ground, no approach has been made to a coalescence of the separated parts. On what principle can this be accounted for, except that the main cause, which produced the division still exists, viz: the more serious and less reconcilable difference on doctrinal subjects?

We admit that one question not pertaining to doctrine interposes a bar to reunion. There are many

Congregational churches in the New-school connection, with reference to which the Presbyteries to which they belong have taken action, guaranteeing to them the permanency of their present relations; and the New-school General Assembly at their last meeting reaffirmed the existence of the Plan of Union; thereby virtually perpetuating Congregationalism in their bounds. It is well known however that many Congregational churches connected with their body have been for years more or less uneasy in their anomalous position; and the course pursued on this subject by the Convention at Albany last autumn, is adapted to increase their uneasiness and to lead them one after another to Independency. It was probably with a view to allay their dissatisfaction and to prevent any movement towards a separate organization, that the New-school Assembly adopted the resolution just referred to. But would they have done this, if they had believed that the chief bar to a reunion with the Old-school Church was the existence of Congregationalism in their own body? Many of them had in different forms intimated their desire for a connection with us, provided they could come in as a body; and they were acquainted with the fact that the Congregational churches under the care of their Presbyteries, so far from feeling themselves bound to continue their connection with those Presbyteries by virtue of the Plan of Union, were now and then becoming Independent; and that for ten years past Congregational editors have been urging upon the people holding their views of church government, to carry out their denominational preferences by organizing themselves into Congregational Associations. Under these circumstances, that Assembly could have easily opened the way (if they had been so disposed) for the voluntary separation of the Congregational churches from their body; without any violation of an existing compact even with their own understanding of its binding force. But the truth was, they were conscious that if this barrier should be removed, there existed another which would render it very difficult, if not impossible, for the Old and New-school divisions to form *collectively* a reunion, without a change in the views of one of the parties. First, the same difference exists as formerly, with regard to what is implied in adopting our Confession of Faith. In a recent work authorized by the Synods of New York and New Jersey, a notice of which is found in our Introduction, the writer acknowledges that the New-school party, which he represents, admits "of diversity of views on points not affecting the integrity of the system," and that "perfect uniformity in reference to a system so comprehensive and minute in its details, is not to be expected, and ought not to be required." In this acknowledgment we have the starting point of the differences between the two schools. The Old-school do require an honest, full and hearty subscription to the creed of the church; the New leaves every one to judge what is essential to the system; and under this convenient subterfuge, the protean forms of new theology have crept into the church. Again, the same difference exists as in former years, on several important points of Scripture doctrine. The extravagant manner of speaking which was then common in some sections of our country is now unknown; and there are indications of a sounder faith in a number of ministers who were once of questionable orthodoxy. But several of those men whose published errors were the main ground of our former troubles, are now in the New-school body, take a prominent and leading part, and maintain and teach the same doctrines as in years past. The Rev. Albert Barnes, as Moderator of the New-school General Assembly of 1851, delivered a discourse before that body, in which he not only reaffirmed his former errors, but caricatured those doctrines which from time immemorial have been esteemed orthodox, and which are known to be held by the Old-school. When a motion was made to print it, one or two members (perhaps more—I write from recollection) expressed their dissent from some points contained in it, and objected to its being published under the sanction of the Assembly. The motion was withdrawn, but with the understanding that the discourse should be printed, which was accordingly done. How many of that Assembly dissented from its teachings I have no means of knowing; but not an individual *protested* against them, or even expressed disapprobation except in the manner above mentioned. We are not aware that the accredited organs of that body contained any strictures on the sermon after it came from the press; and in one section of the country (we cannot speak for all) we happen to know that pains were taken by persons belonging to that church to circulate it among the people. The periodicals alluded to, as for example the Biblical Repository, the New York Evangelist, and the Philadelphia Christian Observer, furnish also positive evidence, from the character of some of their articles, that those errors are held by some, we fear a considerable number, in that connection.

EFFECTS OF THE DIVISION.

The necessity for a division of the church was deprecated by all; and by none more sincerely than the Old-school. It was anticipated that temporary evils and inconveniences would result from it, which no legislation could wholly prevent. But it was deemed preferable to submit to these evils, for the sake of avoiding still greater ones which appeared to be inevitable, if the two parties in the church should continue any longer in the same body. To use the language of an excellent and distinguished brother in the ministry, "We were reduced to this simple question, Is the Presbyterian Church worth an effort to save?" The effort was made, and in the good providence of God it has been crowned with success. Our condition as a Church, we are persuaded, is far better than it would have been if the division had not occurred, unless (an event not to have been expected) our New-school brethren had materially modified their former views.

One beneficial effect of the separation has been the enjoyment of greater *harmony* and *peace*. However humiliating the acknowledgment, it is nevertheless true, that for seven years or more previous to the division, so heterogeneous were the materials which composed the highest judicatory of our church, that the floor of the General Assembly had become an arena of strife and controversy. Irrespective of the question which of the two parties were in the wrong, the simple facts that they were at variance, and that their differences could not be reconciled, were sufficient reasons, as in the case of Abraham and Lot, (Gen. xiii. 8, 9) not only for justifying but demanding separation. The removal of these discordant elements, and the organization of another body by that portion of the church which differed from us, restored to our Assembly that harmony of action which characterized its early history.

Another effect of the division has been the restoration to our body of its former *unity in doctrinal views*. A half century ago it was sufficient to know that a man was a Presbyterian minister, in order to feel assured that he was sound in the faith, according to the Calvinistic sense of this phrase. But for ten years previous to 1837, this test was quite insufficient. Under the Presbyterian name, and with Presbyterian credentials, ministers passed from congregation to congregation in certain parts of our country, and promulgated Arminian and even Pelagian tenets. At the former period, in changing one's ministerial connection from one Presbytery to another, a certificate of good and regular standing was deemed sufficient, without a personal examination. But during the latter, the presenting of "clean papers" was found to be no certain evidence of soundness in the faith. Distrust and suspicion took the place of confidence. Some Presbyteries began to *examine* applicants for admission to their bodies from other Presbyteries, however satisfactory might be their written credentials. This practice being objected to, the question was brought before the General Assembly. In 1834, the right to re-examine was denied. But in 1835, (the Old-school being in the majority,) the Assembly decided that "it is the right of every Presbytery to be entirely satisfied of the soundness in the faith of those ministers who apply to be admitted into the Presbytery as members." This was a partial remedy of the evil; but our former unity of sentiment was not restored, until the separate organization of the New-school body.

The "History of the Division" already referred to, after quoting the Adopting Act of 1729, observes: "This instrument does immortal honour to its authors, and those who receive it as a bond of Christian union and fellowship. It provides for the preservation, 'pure and entire,' of the *system* of doctrine" (the italics are not in the Adopting Act) "embraced in the Confession of Faith and Catechism. To errors which are subversive of this system, it gives not the least approval or even toleration, and at the same time admits what is undoubtedly true of every human symbol of doctrinal belief, equally extensive and minute in its details, that it embraces some things in regard to which those who sincerely adopt it, may lawfully differ. It likewise bound those who adopted it, to treat each other, their minor differences notwithstanding, with Christian courtesy and brotherly affection. It is difficult to conceive how it could have been better adapted to keep 'the unity of the Spirit in the bond of peace.' Had the Presbyterian Church in this country been governed by the pacific and magnanimous principles of this act, she would, at this time, have been a united body." To this last remark we give our assent. It was to preserve the unity which is here so much lauded, that the Old-school made such strenuous efforts before the division of the church. They have not, to my knowledge, either before or since, taken any higher ground than that required by the Adopting Act of 1729. A reference to Chapter X. of this treatise will show that our New-school brethren contended for much greater latitude than was authorized by that act. The errors which they refused to condemn, were believed by their Old-school brethren to be "subversive" of the "system of doctrine embraced in the Confession of Faith and Catechisms;" and hence, according to the author's own showing, that act did "not give them the least approval or even toleration." If the New-school had co-operated with the Old in adopting efficient measures to counteract those errors when they first made their appearance, they might have been rectified without a division, and the church "have been at this time a united body." The truly catholic spirit of the Adopting Act is felt and manifested as heartily and consistently by the Old-school body as the New. The cases alluded to in the "History" for a different purpose, show that there is among us no disposition to place our ministers on the "bed of Procrustes," and require them, on pain of excommunication, to be exactly conformed to this iron model. Uniformity in Christian doctrine is not understood as requiring a perfect agreement in *"minor"* points; but it is equally removed from that false liberality which includes under the head of minor points, important and dangerous errors. The Bible rule is, "first pure, then peaceable." To secure this purity, and the peace that succeeds it, was the end which the Old-school hoped to obtain by the separation; it having become apparent that neither was practicable while the two parties remained together. And as far as we are able to judge by a reference to the past history of the church, there is now as much unity of doctrinal views in the Old-school body as at any former period since the organization of the Presbyterian Church in this country. The present character of the New-school church in this respect, I shall not attempt to describe. At the Auburn Convention in 1837, a prominent member observed to me, "You find us here of all colours;" but I trust they have become more homogeneous in sentiment since that time.

A third result of the division has been the existence of more harmony and efficiency in *benevolent action*. Above a century ago, the work of sending missionaries to our frontier settlements and the Indian tribes received the attention of the church; and simultaneously with this, the education of pious and talented young men for the gospel ministry. The records of old Synods of New York and Philadelphia, before and after the union, show that a great deal was accomplished in these several departments; and after the organization of the General Assembly, in 1789, these objects occupy a prominent place in the minutes of that body. In 1802, the Assembly appointed a Standing Committee of Missions; and in 1817 they constituted the Board of Missions, with enlarged powers and a permanent organization. An overture was sent down to the Presbyteries in 1805, respecting the education of pious youth for the gospel ministry, and action was taken on the subject at the following and one or two subsequent meetings of the Assembly, till 1819, when the Board of Education was constituted, to superintend and carry on this department in behalf of the Assembly. But for some time these Boards were rather bonds of union between the different judicatories of the church, than the sole agents to prosecute the work. Presbyteries and Synods, in many instances, conducted both missions and education in their own bounds, and reported their doings annually, either to the Boards or directly to the Assembly. Important good, however, was accomplished by the direct agency of these Boards, both in training candidates and in sending missionaries to destitute white settlements, to the coloured population of the South, and to different Indian tribes. In 1809, the Assembly adopted a resolution, "earnestly recommending that each Synod take measures for establishing as many religious tract societies within their bounds, by the associating of one or more Presbyteries, as may be most convenient for this purpose."

One such society was subsequently organized by the Synod of Philadelphia, denominated the Presbyterian Tract Society, which published fifteen or twenty valuable tracts, forming two volumes of the series of works now issued by the Assembly's Board of Publication.

The formation of the American Board of Commissioners for Foreign Missions, the American Education Society, the American Home Missionary Society, and the American Tract Society, modified the policy and divided the action of the Presbyterian Church, with regard to these several objects. Except the Synod of Pittsburgh, who carried on the missionary work among several tribes of Indians, our efforts for Foreign Missions were made principally through the American Board. The mission among the Cherokees, which had been commenced by the Committee of Missions appointed by the Assembly, and conducted successfully for seven years, at an expense of eight or ten thousand dollars, was placed under the care of that Board; and the Synods of Virginia and North Carolina formed therewith a direct auxiliary connection; though with the condition incorporated in their constitution, that they might withdraw from it without offence, or a breach of courtesy, whenever the General Assembly should think proper to resume the work of Foreign Missions. The American Education Society had a Presbyterian Branch, and the American Tract and Home Missionary Societies were allowed free access to our churches for the collection of funds to carry on their operations. In the department of Domestic Missions and Ministerial Education, for the promotion of which our own Boards were operating at the same time, difficulties and collisions were found to result from the action of two independent organizations for these objects in the same field, to say nothing of the doctrinal errors which were incidentally introduced among us through the operation of those societies. The action of our Boards was restrained and embarrassed, and far less was accomplished than would have been under more favorable circumstances. This was one source of the difficulty between the two parties in the church, some particulars of which have been already given. The resolutions adopted by the last New-school Assembly on this subject, are a virtual admission that the Old-school were right in that contest. Since the division, these four objects, viz: Domestic Missions, Foreign Missions, Ministerial and General Education, and the Publication of Evangelical Books and Tracts, have been all conducted by as many distinct but co-ordinate Boards, under the supervision of the General Assembly. We regard them as wisely adapted to accomplish the ends which they have in view. For harmony and energy in action, for efficiency and usefulness in their results, they are unsurpassed by any similar organizations in our country. Next to the stated ministry of the gospel, they constitute the power and glory of our church. Their success and usefulness afford pleasing evidence of the divine favour. Yes! I record it, not with boasting, but gratitude, that (as I verily believe) the Holy Spirit is with these Boards of the church, and that the providence of God is over them—the former to impart to them unity and vitality; the latter to defend and prosper them:—as in Ezekiel's vision of the four wheels, (i. 15—28) whose co-ordinate and involved movements were regular, harmonious, and constant, receiving their impetus from an invisible spirit within them, while above, directing and controling the whole, appeared the enthroned Redeemer, encircled with the bow of covenant love. We have now no pretext for inaction. While we rejoice in the zeal and success of every branch of Christ's church who are engaged in promoting his cause, let us not be behind them, either in the expansiveness or efficiency of our benevolence.

Finally; we have enjoyed as a church greater *prosperity* and *enlargement* since the division, than could have been reasonably anticipated, if the two parties had continued together. Had there been a unanimity of sentiment in the whole church, our growth, like that of our nation, might have been constant; and our prosperity increased rather than diminished, by preserving the integrity of the body, and "consecrating our united energies to the advancement of Christ's kingdom." But we were virtually divided, for several years before the organization of two separate bodies—divided in sentiment though nominally acting in concert. Under these circumstances, a merely nominal union added nothing either to the beauty or strength of the church; and our continuance in the same body gave no promise of future prosperity. After the separation, each party was in a position to act more unitedly and efficiently than before. We have since experienced no hinderance from our New-school brethren or they from us. As to which of the two bodies has enjoyed *greater* prosperity, or received a *larger* number to its communion, we shall make no particular estimate. Comparisons of this kind may be regarded as invidious; and besides, numerical increase is not a sure test of the divine approbation. But so far as an appeal to this circumstance is admissible, we have abundant reason to be satisfied and thankful to God for our present relative position. A detailed statistical account would show that in the increase of numbers, in the extension of territory, and in whatever else constitutes external prosperity we have made great and pleasing progress. But in the present connection I am not disposed to particularize. There is an apostolic caution, "Be not high minded but fear." Since we are so highly favoured in outward circumstances, let it be our earnest prayer and diligent effort to enjoy in an equal degree *internal* prosperity. Our growth in *grace* and *holiness* should be in grand parallel with our progress in numbers and influence.

PROPER TREATMENT OF EACH OTHER.

As we are now two distinct bodies, it is obvious that the same principles should govern us in our intercourse with each other, as are applicable to all evangelical churches. The circumstance that we have recently been one church, has a tendency (such is human nature) to make us more cold in exchanging ordinary Christian courtesies, than we should be, if we had never belonged to the same body. This tendency has been counteracted, in a great degree, by the lapse of fifteen years; and it will be ere long removed, unless a vindictive and jealous spirit is fostered and kept alive by those who control public sentiment. The Old-school, as far as I am acquainted, are generally disposed to treat their New-school brethren with kindness; to throw no obstacle in the way of their prosperity; to hold with them occasional communion; to supply their pulpits when invited, and to extend to their ministers who may be known to be sound in the faith, ministerial fellowship and confidence. These feelings are reciprocated by some of the New-school body. But others among them continue to reiterate, in censorious and even abusive language, the charge of injustice and oppression, in the measures adopted by the General Assembly of 1837, to accuse us of an intolerant and bigoted spirit in not now consenting to a reunion of the two bodies, and yet insinuate that we contemplate a union at no distant day, by the " absorption of their ministers and churches." We refer to these things, not to discuss their merits, but for the purpose of remarking, (1) that it is a singular preparation for reunion, to abuse the party with whom it is proposed to unite; (2) that if we were to form a reunion, and if such a spirit as is here manifested *towards* the Old-school body should be exhibited *within* it, a second division would be as necessary as the first; (3) that when the chief causes which produced the separation shall cease to exist, the Old-school church will unquestionably be as cordial in listening to an overture for reunion from the New-school division, as they always have been when receiving similar applications from other churches of the same faith and order with ourselves; (4) that we never have been distinguished as a *proselyting* church, are not so now, and of course are not accustomed to make any attempts to "absorb the ministers and churches" of other denominations; yet we always open our doors to receive those, whether ministers, churches, or individual members, who embrace the doctrines contained in our standards, and express a desire to enter our communion; (5) that though for a number of years before the separation, we were unhappily too often coming into collision, it becomes us now to lay aside former jealousies, and "study the things which make for peace." There is no good reason why "Ephraim should envy Judah, or Judah vex Ephraim."

It is on the whole no disadvantage that there are different Christian denominations. The numerical unity of the Papal church, or even its boasted unity of religious faith, is very dissimilar to the catholic unity which is commended and enjoined in the Holy Scriptures. The Reformed churches in the days of Luther and Calvin, Cranmer and Knox, though not in every respect identical in creed, form of government, or mode of worship, were characterized by as much real unity as though they had all acknowledged one visible head; and they probably acted with greater efficiency in their varied yet concurring efforts to advance the Redeemer's kingdom. The same may be true now; and hence it should be regarded as an object of less importance to secure an organic union of all evangelical churches in the same body, than to see them all faithfully and zealously performing the work of the Lord under their own banners; while towards each other they keep "the unity of the Spirit in the bond of peace." This idea carried out to perfection, with the additional one of the glorious presence of Christ with his people, contains the chief elements in those sublime descriptions recorded in God's word, of the future state of the Church during her best and brightest period on earth.

THE END.

Date Loaned

Demco 292-5

Wood
AUTHOR
Doctrinal Differences
TITLE

509

DATE LOANED	BORR
6/19/58	

**The Library
Union Theological Seminary**
Broadway at 120th Street
New York 27, N. Y.

Check Out More Titles From HardPress Classics Series In this collection we are offering thousands of classic and hard to find books. This series spans a vast array of subjects – so you are bound to find something of interest to enjoy reading and learning about.

Subjects:
Architecture
Art
Biography & Autobiography
Body, Mind &Spirit
Children & Young Adult
Dramas
Education
Fiction
History
Language Arts & Disciplines
Law
Literary Collections
Music
Poetry
Psychology
Science
…and many more.

Visit us at www.hardpress.net

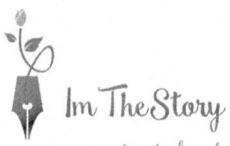

Im The Story
personalised classic books

"Beautiful gift.. lovely finish.
My Niece loves it, so precious!"

Helen R Brumfieldon

★★★★★

UNIQUE GIFT

FOR KIDS, PARTNERS
AND FRIENDS

Timeless books such as:

Kids

Alice in Wonderland • The Jungle Book • The Wonderful Wizard of Oz
Peter and Wendy • Robin Hood • The Prince and The Pauper
The Railway Children • Treasure Island • A Christmas Carol

Adults

Romeo and Juliet • Dracula

Highly Customizable • **Change** Books Title • **Replace** Characters Names with yours • **Upload** Photo (for inside page) • **Add** Inscriptions

Visit
ImTheStory.com
and order yours today!

WS - #0143 - 190126 - C0 - 229/152/18 - PB - 9780371875926 - Gloss Lamination